Who Flapped Their Wings

A Collection of Awe Inspiring Stories

by Dorna Djenab

ISBN 978-1-0682300-7-3

To the Beloved – as Hafiz & Rumi, the Persian mystics, would call it
who is Everything, Everywhere and always Here.
My ultimate compass.
The light which guides my way.

To all my ancestors including my grandparents
who showered unconditional love and with whom I felt safe.

To my parents, Mahvash and Fereydoun
for their commitment to creativity and excellence
and for teaching me the most sacred foundation of life on earth.

To my daughter, Donya
for her gentleness and warmth
and for the joy in her eyes when she sees me do what I love.
May she always remember that **seeing miracles is a choice**.

To my other half, Matt
for his generous spirit, his faith in me
and for always providing the space and support to explore and develop my ideas.

To my brother, Arash
for his kindness, attention to details, continual encouragement
and for being my honest critic.

To all my friends and students
for their presence
and who, over the years, have *seen* me and rooted for my growth.

Table of Contents

Acknowledgment

A heartfelt thank you to everyone who shared their stories with me – whether in writing, voice notes, or conversation. Not all stories made it into this book, but every single one contributed to its spirit and helped strengthen my intention to write it. Without your openness, generosity and willingness to share something so personal, this book would not exist. You trusted me with your encounters with mystery and in doing so, allowed these moments to touch the hearts of others. I am deeply grateful for your kindness.

A special thanks to Matt Gluck and Suzanne Sive for editing the final copy and showing me that even after 36 years of living in England, I still make mistakes :)

To my mother Mahvash, my brother Arash, my daughter Donya, my other half Matt, my close friends (you know who you are), for listening to my stories as I was writing.
Your reactions kept me going!

Introduction

~ There are only two ways to live your life. One is as though nothing is a miracle. The other is as though everything is a miracle
~ Albert Einstein ~

Even today, at the age of 55, a mysterious experience I had in my teenage years – while I was trying to help my father – blows me away. Deep down, I believe this experience changed me and my worldview for good. What happened felt as though an invisible force had pierced through a veil between this world and an unseen realm, just to help me. It did a lot more than that though: It showed my ignorance of the depth of life's mystery. It revealed a direct and intimate connection between me and something mighty and deeply loving. This unseen *power* wasn't summoned at will and I don't believe it can be but, I understood that it was as intimately close to me as I am to myself. It was impossible for me to deny that there was more to me than the eye could see. During those turbulent teenage years, while my country – Iran – was at war and everything seemed grim, this realisation was priceless. Despite the impact of this and similar events throughout my life, they eventually faded into the background and were forgotten.

In a book by Carlos Castaneda that I read five years before sitting down to write this book, Don Juan, a spiritual healer, a Yaqui shaman, asks his student – Carlos Castaneda – to create an inventory of his meaningful life's events as part of a process of self-examination and personal transformation. After reading that chapter, I decided to make my own list. As I was writing the list of events, I realised they were all mysterious coincidences I had experienced – including the one mentioned above. Remembering each and every one of them filled me, once again, with the sense of being supported by and connected to a great mystery that transcends human understanding.

At the time of this exercise, I wasn't particularly low, but I was certainly going through significant changes in many aspects of my life. I felt both excitement and fear as I moved towards the unknown. It was certainly timely to vividly remember the mysterious stories within my life story and to be reminded of powerful and invisible resources that could emerge out of nowhere.

I had a thought: if revisiting these experiences could boost me with confidence, courage and calm amidst challenges, it could do the same for others.

The idea of this book was born and I began reaching out to everyone I met, eager to hear if they had such stories. While many found it easy to recall their experiences, they confessed to never having shared them before. Some wanted to protect the sacredness of such intimate events, while others feared judgement, being doubted or dismissed. In some cases, there was an initial hesitancy, an undertone of denial of the impact even, but as they shared their stories, excitement grew and wonder flowed through our conversations. As it turned out, not everyone has had such experiences; some had only one powerful event to share while a few people seemed *prone* to them.

It was a real privilege to listen to these stories and witness the immediate change in the mood of the story-teller and the spark it created in their whole being. One moment before sharing, they may have sounded a bit down, lacking energy and not really enthused by life and the next, they would be excited, inspired and filled with a zest for life. This enlivening was exactly what I had hoped for.

During these conversations, certain questions kept coming up: Are these experiences merely the products of our imagination? Is it at all possible that they are completely random? Are we desperately seeking something powerful to rely on, as we navigate the challenges of loss, conflicts and change? The truth is, we don't have a definitive answer and it's likely we never will. However, what we do know is that the depth and intensity of the feelings surrounding these chance happenings are unlike anything we've ever experienced.

This book is a collection of awe-inspiring stories, meant to spark a deep sense of wonder about existence. It is also an invitation to consider a profound question: 'Is there more to us than we 'know'?' Perhaps, while reading, forgotten memories will resurface or long-held certainties will be gently questioned. Even if these questions don't lead to deeper understanding right away, holding them – with an open mind – may do so in time. One thing is certain: without curiosity and a thirst for truth, humanity would not have discovered as much as it has. As Stephen Hawking eloquently said:
'The greatest enemy of knowledge is not ignorance, it is the illusion of knowledge.'

There are only three stories in the entire book, whose source I didn't know personally, but came through the personal network as a recorded message. All the other stories have been given to me directly or are my own. Some were typed or shared via voice messages, while others were spoken. I've taken the liberty of rewriting and refining them to capture both the factual details and emotional content, keeping some of the original names and changing others.

In the following pages, you will find stories that are familiar and easy to relate to. However, some stories have a surreal tone and the turn of events seem harder to believe. Ultimately, what brings these stories to these pages is the transformative effects they had on those who shared them and whose only gain is to spread the awe, the light and what made their hair tingle. Albert Einstein once said:

'The most beautiful thing we can experience is the mysterious.'

So, let the journey to and through the mystery begin!

Elusive Power

This happened in Tehran when I was around 16 or 17 years old. I don't remember the exact year but it was during the Iran-Iraq war so maybe 1985 or '86. As in any war, food was rationed, poverty spread fast and on top of that, the political and social oppression in the country was at its peak. We lived under circumstances that fuelled insecurity and anxiety throughout. On the surface we went with the flow. Underneath though, the fear of 'openly' doing anything disapproved of by the Islamic law entrapped us, knowing it could lead to imprisonment and even harsh punishment.

We were also constantly reminded of our own impermanent nature. The thick tape strips on windows, meant to stop flying glass during missile strikes, were a clear sign of imminent danger. The dreadful sounds of warning sirens and the panicked screams of neighbours quickly evacuating their flats to find refuge in the basement during the total blackouts, had become part of our 'normal' life. On a level, I consider myself lucky that my parents, open to their fate, chose for us to stay home in our flat on the fourth floor and not rush down as the sirens wailed. The only time that we did, was enough for my parents to decide that it was easier to surrender to a potential catastrophe in the comfort of our own home, instead of amidst the cries of neighbours and their distressed prayers.

Normal life and routines had to carry on though and as such, most Fridays (equivalent to Sundays in the West) we would go to my grandparents for lunch and leave around dusk. On this particular Friday, we stopped on the way to get some freshly baked stone oven bread. My father and I got out of the car and stood in the queue to be served. I loved watching the flames flicker and dance in the oven and smell the freshly baked bread. The contrasting warmth in the cold winter brought a subtle vibe of safety all around. My father was distant though, he seemed low and lost in his thoughts as was often the case when his depression would flare. We bought our bread and came back to the car to join my mother and younger brother.

We arrived home a couple of minutes later. As we were getting out of the car, my father gasped in horror: 'I've lost my bag!' Panic gripped him as he remembered that his small man bag contained his money, keys, driving licence and if I recall correctly, even his birth certificate. We all suggested that it might have fallen into the roadside stream next to where we had parked by the bakery. 'We will find it' I said, hoping that my optimistic tone would ease his growing sense of despair. The two of us headed back, hopeful to find his bag right where we had parked. Alas, there was no sign of it.

Night had fallen by this time and it became pitch black. We relied on the car's headlights, starting and stopping as we followed the stream, carefully searching one small area at a time. We arrived at a filter zone where only water could flow through, leaving everything else behind. If the bag had been carried by the water, we would have found it there. There was no trace of it and as desperate as I was, I couldn't stay hopeful.

I caught a glimpse of my father's face. He was distraught. The anticipation of replacing his lost belongings weighed heavily on him. Every task from getting new keys to obtaining a new driving licence seemed unbearable, intensified by his condition. Witnessing the pain of the man who always understood and loved me unconditionally broke my heart. In that moment, nothing mattered more to me than being able to help him and take away his burden.
I desperately wished I could find his bag.

With long faces, we both got in the car and started our journey back home. I couldn't bear seeing him in that state. I thought 'there just has to be a way! Maybe we didn't search well enough.'

As I was lost in these thoughts, suddenly, out of nowhere, without even intending to, I slammed my hands on the dashboard and yelled 'STOP!'
What was happening? Why did I do that? I had no idea. Surprised by my sudden urgency, he stopped the car. I got out, crossed the road and approached the stream. Leaning down, I saw my arm reach into the water as if of its own accord, with a purpose, like it knew what it was doing. I emphasise that I was not consciously deciding to extend my arm, I was witnessing its action and that in itself, felt surreal.
Was it reaching for the bag? It couldn't possibly be, as we had scanned the stream carefully. Suddenly, my eyes caught sight of what my hand was reaching towards. Was I dreaming?
I picked it up, soaked and undeniably my father's bag.

The emotions that flooded through me were indescribable. Yes, I was overjoyed to have found his bag but this joy had a quality I had never experienced before – it was surreal. Back in the car, I handed him the bag with a beaming smile. He looked as stunned as I felt and asked,
'How did you know?'
All I managed to utter was a quiet 'I don't know.'
A beautiful silence wrapped us both as we drove home. We were speechless and needed time to process the immensity of what had just happened.

My mind was blown away by the elusive power that gifted itself to me when I desperately needed it. This experience showed me that I was part of something bigger, more powerful – a vast cosmic body that responds, supports and communicates with its cells. This realisation became the very foundation on which I built my life today.

I'm fully aware that my experience is not proof that a mechanistic and materialistic worldview is too limited compared to what *is*. Since then though, to continue to cling to a sense of separateness was no longer an option for me. It would have felt disloyal to whatever it was that made me stop the car and my father's suffering.

The Words That Came

I was in my late teens when my father was diagnosed with colon cancer. A strong man in every way, he was a role model to both me and my younger brother. For the next five years, we watched as he faced the challenges of his illness with courage, never once complaining. My mother stood by his side like a pillar of strength, managing both the household and their business. Deep down, we knew it was unlikely our father would survive and as teenagers, that made our own struggles even harder to bear.

For years, I had worked in my parents' travel agency and had learned a lot about the business. In my early twenties, I moved out and took a job elsewhere – at an airline company.

All my colleagues knew my father was unwell and those who cared would often ask how he was doing. One morning, a female colleague asked about him and the words that came out of my mouth shocked me. For no reason whatsoever, I said: 'My father died last night.'
Why did I say that? Had something happened? Did I unconsciously want his suffering to end? I couldn't believe myself.

Only a couple of hours later, I received a phone call. Our father, Michael, had passed away.

I often look back at that moment, never understanding what compelled me to say those words. Did an unconscious part of me know what was about to happen and try to prepare me? Was it my father himself telling me he was gone? Whatever mystery caused it, I was unknowingly more prepared for the news, as I had already given it to someone else.

Ashes in the River

I met Caroline in Amsterdam while waiting for the Eurostar train on our way back to London. My partner and brother were searching for a place to sit in the overcrowded station. After several days of walking around the city, there was no way we were going to stand for another two hours while waiting for the train. I scanned the area hoping to find a spot for us to sit. Unfortunately, all the available seats were taken and many passengers were already sitting on the floor. There were a few bench tables and I looked closely to see if we could find some space there. Luckily, we're not shy and had no problem sharing a table with strangers.

I spotted a table with six seats where only two people were sitting, engaged in conversation. It was a lady in her sixties and a young man. I assumed them to be mother and son and approached them. They were both super friendly and warm and happily made room for us to sit. Soon after, we were all engrossed in deep and meaningful conversation. As it turned out, they weren't mother and son after all; in fact, they were total strangers. Their friendly demeanour had given the impression of a strong bond between them. Caroline was very motherly and wrapped her arms around mine as we shared the delight of our newfound bond. What a blessing it is to meet such lovely people while traveling, especially in an incredibly busy train station where you can meet all sorts of folk! Time flew by and we were surprised when the announcement came that our train had arrived and it was time to board. We said our goodbyes, expressing our gratitude for this wonderful meeting.

We sat in Coach 13, around a table together. Our seat numbers were 53, 54 and 57. To my surprise, I spotted Caroline in the same coach, searching for her seat. I was even more surprised to learn that her seat number was 58 and she was meant to sit at our table! What were the odds of that? Out of about 200 passengers, over 30 bench tables and many single seats in the train station, I had chosen to sit next to the person who would share the journey with us on the train all the way back to London! While our encounter could be a story on its own, this one is about Caroline's. She shared it with us when she discovered that I was collecting stories that stop us in our tracks and make us ponder the mysteries of life.

Here is what she told us:

Four years ago, my mother passed away. A few years before that she had considered asking for euthanasia to end her life and to declare her decision, she had gathered us all – her five children – at her favourite restaurant by the water. She loved that place surrounded by natural beauty where instead of the city noise, the murmurs of a river nearby could be heard.

We were all saddened by the news that she wanted to leave this world but also knew we couldn't persuade her otherwise. We also knew that she hadn't even seen the doctors about it and that ultimately, it was them who would need to approve the procedure. Given her decision could be rejected, we decided to make the best of the time we all had together. We had some drinks and as usual we – the children – enjoyed our beers and she had a glass of white wine.

Even though euthanasia is legal where we live in Holland, the medical authorities are very strict about who can undergo the procedure. These decisions are not taken lightly and there is an entire protocol around it. My mother had believed that because she was a member of a particular group, she could request it whenever she wanted, just like ordering food at McDonald's. She had planned all the details to the point of asking it to be scheduled on a Monday as to not inconvenience the doctors over the weekend. Luckily for us the doctors refused her request as she was too well and fit for them to let her end her life.

In the end, my mother lived to be 95 content that she had lived a full life and ready to move on. She received palliative sedation to stop her eating and drinking and was given morphine to alleviate her pain. She peacefully passed away and her life was celebrated during a beautiful ceremony that we held for her in a pub. We were moved as we witnessed the love and the support of 200 friends and family who attended.

My siblings and I collected her ashes afterwards and decided to go to her favourite restaurant and release them, discretely, into the river next to it that she loved. We then went inside to have a drink in her memory. We ordered five beers as per our family tradition, so when the waitress came with the tray of drinks we were stunned. What she brought to our table was five beers and an additional glass of white wine which we hadn't ordered. White wine was my mother's favourite drink!

It was a full-blown goosebumps moment!
For us, it was clear that she was making her presence known.

Remembering this special story still gives me a sense of warmth, knowing wherever she is, she can still show her sense of humour.

African Spirituality

I was eager to learn more about African spirituality and having roots in Africa, I knew that there was a wealth of spiritual wisdom there that hadn't yet found its way into mainstream consciousness. I wanted to focus my attention to its discovery, as up until then most of my research had led me to spiritual thoughts with Eastern origin. I began my exploration and finally after a lot of research, I found an African spiritual group based in London. When I reached out to them, they were incredibly kind over the phone, leaving me with a positive impression. Intrigued, I thought it would be nice to attend one of their services and get to know them better. During a later conversation, they explained their onboarding process. All prospective members interested in joining the community had to undergo a specific type of psychic reading so that they could ascertain their personality, vibe and whether or not they would fit in with the group. They described the community as a tight-knit family, very protective of one another and the reading was to make sure that whoever joins is trustworthy.

I understood and agreed to have the reading done. Everything went smoothly and it felt right. They reassured me that I had passed the process and they were very happy with how I came across. I seemed to have the right 'energy'. However, after their initial positive response, the communication no longer flowed and they were slow and unresponsive to my follow-up messages. In spite of that, my eagerness to join them wasn't diminished for the first few months. Eventually though, when I heard nothing back despite my persistent attempts to get a response, my enthusiasm dried out and I totally forgot about my application.

Then one day, out of nowhere, a thought crossed my mind. I remembered that one of my spiritual teachers who's like an aunty to me, believes that Spirit communicates in various ways, including through numbers. She is a fascinating lady and I am very fond of her.

She tells me the number 1111 holds great significance for her, symbolising new beginnings and being on the right track. Coincidentally, even her bank's sort code includes 1111. If numbers are means through which Spirit communicates, I pondered, surely, it could also use certain numbers as warning signs – like those with negative associations, such as 911, 999 or, 666.

Only a few seconds into this very random thought, my phone pinged. I was very surprised to see that I had finally received a text from the lady I had spoken with about joining the African spiritual group. It had been months since our last conversation. She thanked me for undergoing the reading and gave me her bank account details for the payment, so that I could finally attend their service. I was taken aback by her bank account number which contained 999 – the emergency call number in the UK. How could my spontaneous thoughts about warning messages with numbers coincide so precisely with receiving her text? My attention was drawn to the number sequence on the account details only because of a random thought a few seconds before. I would have otherwise not even noticed 999, let alone thought much of it. Given this unexpected and awkward coincidence, I decided to err on the side of caution and take it as a warning sign. Even though I couldn't find a logical explanation, I couldn't find myself joining them as doubt had now replaced my initial excitement. As eager as I had been to join them, my enthusiasm was in no way stronger than the power of this undeniable, unexpected coincidence.
I thanked her, paid for the reading but never looked back.

Keep Going

Back in 2024, on a flight back to London from a holiday in Cambodia, I slept in an awkward position, triggering an unbearable sciatic episode. Generally, I consider myself to be fit and active, regularly going to the gym. I had been fortunate up until then (I was 59 at the time), not to have experienced such excruciating pain due to a pinched nerve. This experience was however truly debilitating. To make matters worse, my job involves sitting all day at a desk, dealing with very stressful and time sensitive issues. One week later, there were no signs of any improvement and the pain persisted. After only a few steps I would freeze. I couldn't put any weight on my leg without wanting to scream. What would normally be a two-minute walk took me 15 minutes. I didn't know what to do. I knew it was time to have it checked, as it didn't seem to be healing on its own.

That day after work, I was going for a massage treatment. I was in a lot of pain and had to 'will' myself towards my car. As I was walking, the pain was so intense that tears welled in my eyes. I looked ahead to see how far I had to go still. Then, as if it was there just for me, I saw it. On the pavement, written in thick, bold chalk letters:
KEEP GOING!
I have no idea why someone would have written that on a paving slab on a random street.

I cannot put into words what I felt in that moment. I wasn't alone anymore. My pain was witnessed and I was encouraged to bear it and carry on. It was all that it took for me to take my next step. For some reason, even though the physical pain hadn't vanished, I was able to walk with more confidence. The strength of the message had penetrated my mind and heart, turning me in one instant from a victim to a warrior.

KEEP GOING! I carry this message with me now and will remember it for the rest of my days.

A Timely Hug

Although my partner was a good man, our relationship didn't feel harmonious; it seemed that no matter how hard I tried, I couldn't shake the feeling of incompatibility. Have you heard the expression, 'when the shoe fits, the foot is forgotten'? Well, that never applied to us. There was always a niggling sensation indicating that something was not quite right. Instead of a sense of belonging, true comfort and ease that I wished I shared with my partner, there was always an undercurrent of sadness and discontent in my heart.

I often questioned why I stayed. What was it that held me back, preventing me from breaking free? I yearned to experience, once again, the happiness I had known before meeting him. So, why did I cling day after day, hoping for a miraculous transformation of our relationship into a loving and nourishing one? Was I afraid of being alone or was I afraid of ending up in a worse relationship?

My lack of clarity and inability to take action frustrated me and I grew angry at myself for letting each day slip, not accepting reality and making the necessary changes.

I felt particularly trapped, even on this glorious day in Ibiza where we'd gone on holiday. All I really wanted was to be understood, to be hugged and to feel the joy of real connection. But even while we were away from our normal routine, that feeling was still absent. I went for a walk on the beach by myself, lost in profound melancholy. A sense of loneliness engulfed me and I found myself asking for help as I quietly prayed for a catalyst that would help me make a decision once and for all. The thought that followed was: 'If I am meant to leave my partner, someone on this beach will come and give me a hug.' I immediately realised how strangely specific this thought was.

Within minutes, I noticed a handsome man walking in my direction with an aura of joy and openness. He came directly towards me, gave me the warmest, most heartfelt hug and reassuringly said, 'Don't be sad, it's all going to be alright.' What? I was baffled, almost spooked as he seemed to have read my thoughts as if they were written on my forehead. How uncanny! I stood motionless and awestruck. Had I entered a different dimension, a magical one where all needs were met and every wish came true in an instant?

I had sought a specific sign, something so unique and far-fetched that when it did happen, I knew I was being given the courage I needed to finally leave my partner of 12 years. It felt surreal, almost like a dream. Even today, I want to pinch myself to make sure that my current life is real. I have difficulty believing that I am happily married to the most beautiful soul who loves, cares and still hugs me with the same joy and affection as he did on that unforgettable day by the beach in Ibiza.

Call Her

I have a close friend, Sabine, who, like me, is also a dentist. Typically, we talk every morning over the phone on our way to work. On the weekends though, we tend not to disturb each other's family time, as we both respect those precious moments.

One Saturday afternoon, while driving with my children, I felt a twist in my guts – a deep knowing and a strong urge to call her. I knew I had to, despite our unspoken agreement to avoid weekend calls. I couldn't ignore this visceral call for action, so I phoned her (hands-free, of course). When she answered, she sounded distressed and in pain. It turned out that she had just fallen on a slippery metal plate at the petrol station and was waiting for paramedics. Luckily, she had managed to call them straight away as her phone was in her pocket. She felt relieved, supported and grateful for my call. We were both humbled by the inexplicable force that moved me to call her, even on a Saturday. I stayed with her on the phone until the ambulance arrived to take her to the hospital where she was admitted for a few days. I called her every morning on the way to work until she was discharged.

Every time I recall the experience, I feel immense gratitude to have been there, holding space for her to express her pain and discomfort. The fact that my body knew something had happened is still beyond me but, it was a knowing so powerful and unusual that it was impossible to deny.

We have both felt even closer since, realising that something beyond the physical binds us strongly together. How else could we otherwise explain that I was able to feel her despair through the ether and call her precisely when she needed emotional support?

Public Phone

In 1994, I was 13 years old and in year eight. The previous year, my parents and I had immigrated from Iran due to the political unrest, forced to leave behind loved ones. I was lucky enough to end up at the same new school as Sarah – another Iranian girl, two years older, who was in a similar situation.

Halfway through the year, a boy named Mehdi joined our school. He had recently moved from Iran due to his father's work commitments and spoke very little English. Our shared circumstances made us bond quickly and the three of us became close friends. However, towards the end of the year, Mehdi broke the news that he wouldn't be returning for the next school term. His father's secondment was ending and he and his family were moving back to Iran.

We were all heartbroken at the thought of losing the deep friendship we had formed. Sarah and I bought him a goodbye gift and agreed to visit him and give him his present before he left. When the day came, my uncle kindly agreed to take us to see him. We had never been to his house before. After finding directions in the A to Z map (A street atlas of London), we set off on our journey.

Unfortunately, after an hour of driving around following the map, we were unable to find Mehdi's house. My uncle stopped near a telephone box and asked us to call Mehdi for directions. Sarah and I jumped out and entered the telephone box. As we were preparing our coins and getting the number to call, the public phone rang.

Sarah picked it up and looked at me in shock and disbelief, 'it's Mehdi' she whispered. You might think he saw us from his house, knew the number of the public phone and called us to help us find him. But no, it turned out he was trying to call someone else, misdialed the last digit and ended up calling the exact phone box we were standing in. Once we processed the shock of what had just happened, we managed to get the directions from him and came back to the car. Nervously laughing, we told the story to my uncle who never believed us.

For Sarah and I though, this was an event never to forget. Even now as I recall it, my hair stands on end in awe at the mystery of that day's turn of events. I wanted to tell everyone and pass on the same sense of wonder but I doubted anyone would take me seriously. So, in the fear of having something so magical be scoffed at, up until now, I had not shared this with a soul.

Number Plates

It was a winter afternoon in February 2024 when I visited Five Oaks – a residential care home in Greater London. Most of their residents were elderly people suffering from dementia, Alzheimer's, strokes, or accidents that had left them in need of extra support.

It was my first time there, offering gentle massages to those willing to receive a few minutes of tender, loving care. As always, being with vulnerable people filled me with compassion and I did my best to bring some light and humour to their day. Most of those I met were receptive and seemed to enjoy their sessions, generously giving back through their kind words and appreciation.

I left with mixed emotions: love, sadness, joy, gratitude, compassion and even guilt – for not being able to do the same for my own father, who lives in another country. Despite this range of feelings, love and gratitude were, without a doubt, the most prominent. I was deeply grateful to have played a small part in bringing some moments of comfort to these beautiful old souls.

As I drove while smiling to myself, seeing their many faces in my mind's eye, a van pulled in front of me at a roundabout. I couldn't believe the synchronicity: the registration number ended with **5 OAK**, the very name of the care home I'd just visited. As soon as I stopped at a red light I just had to take a photo!

A burst of pure joy filled me from head to toe! This felt like a wink from the universe – a sign, perhaps, that I was not alone in my thoughts and feelings. It seemed that I was part of a unified symphony of interconnected and harmonious events.
What a gift from a random van!

This had such a wonderful effect on me that, when I spoke to my daughter a few days later, I shared the story. I knew it would fill her with a sense of wonder and give her some much-needed energy. She was exhausted after an 18-hour journey from Zanzibar to Rome, where she had stopped for a night before an early flight home to Ibiza. When we spoke, she was on her way to a restaurant for a meal. We talked until her food arrived, then said goodbye.

An hour later, she sent me a voice message and a photo she'd just taken – a number plate on a black Citroën. It showed our exact current postcode in the UK, with only one extra zero in the middle.
For privacy reasons, I have changed the numbers, but to illustrate the strangeness of this coincidence:

EN305LV – The number plate

EN3 5LV – Our current postcode
As if this wasn't strange enough, when I heard the rest of my daughter's voice message, I laughed out loud. She pointed out that the number plate was our current postcode along with all the digits from our previous one:

EN5 0LV – Our previous postcode

Admittedly, this raises many questions. Does our brain scan for what we are drawn to? Out of the endless stream of data that it processes every moment, does our mind filter out and highlight only what resonates with us? It seems that this is, in fact, the case. It even has a name: the Baader-Meinhoff phenomenon or frequency illusion. Our minds direct our focus to what stimulates our curiosity and filter out the rest. This is why when we learn something new, like a new word, it seems to appear everywhere. Still, this doesn't explain how odd it was to spot our exact postcode on a number plate.
Even if I tried my hardest and I have tried since, I would struggle to find the digits of familiar postcodes, let alone the exact sequence.

How was it that, on an evening in a strange country, on the very night my daughter needed a boost, after hearing my story of the number plate, this peculiar synchronicity took place?
I am certainly left with more food for thought.

Scent of my grandmother

I was six years old when my parents decided to immigrate to France after the unrest of the Iranian Revolution in 1979. My emotional bonds to my family were very strong and I was particularly close to my grandmother, Ra'na joon. She always treated her three granddaughters the same, for example, buying us identical presents to avoid any jealousy amongst us. Even though she never knowingly showed favouritism, everyone felt that I was her favourite granddaughter. Being the youngest at the time might have played a role, so I'm told.

To say that the immigration was traumatic for me would be an understatement. I never experienced that same sense of belonging and warmth that I had felt before our permanent move. With every day that passed, I missed everyone more and more, especially my grandmother. Attending a French school in Iran, the regular short visits to France and my fluency in the language were not enough for a smooth adaptation. I was still ill-equipped to deal with the long, cold and lonely winters in Strasbourg. My parents had good intentions and wanted to give us a better life, sparing us from the oppression of the Islamic regime. However, they never anticipated how daunting the separation from our loved ones would be. We all changed and even they were never the same. To this day, I can still see the nostalgia in their faces and hear it in their voices when they talk about their homeland. It is clear that in an ideal world, they would have never left.

Years passed and even though we were safe in France, away from the missiles and terror of the Iran/Iraq war, we had our own battles to fight. For instance, when my mother had a brain aneurysm, we didn't have the strong supportive community that we would have had back at home. It was a particularly tough period for us all. My father took care of her and made sure that my sister and I did well in our studies.

I could sense his anxiety and her deep sadness and like a sponge, I absorbed everything that they felt.

Since then, I've revisited Iran only about five times, partly due to the political situation and partly because it became harder to say goodbye and return to our isolated life. I couldn't tolerate the heartbreak of leaving, especially since it took longer each time to readjust to the loneliness, particularly after receiving so much love, warmth and attention.

When I was 28, having become a practicing dentist by then, we had some terrible news.

I remember it as if it was yesterday. It was a Monday in October 2001. While my father and I were working in our dental clinic, we received a phone call. It was my uncle, he sounded distressed and shocked as he announced the unexpected death of my beloved grandmother. The joy of my heart, the anchor to the sweet memories of my childhood, was gone. She'd been in hospital for an operation and when she returned home, she took a nap for a quick rest and never woke up.

She'd left me, without a goodbye, without saying a word, without a sign!

I was distraught. On Tuesday, my parents left for the funeral while I mourned from a distance. Work commitments didn't allow both my father and I to leave the clinic unattended at the same time.

Ra'na joon only wore one perfume, She used to say to me: 'A woman should choose one perfume and only wear that.' Hers was a strong yet warm scent, just like her, which she applied practically every day after showering. In all the years I had lived in France, I had never smelled it on anyone. On Wednesday, a patient came for treatment and lo and behold, the room was filled with my grandmother's scent wrapping me in a warm hug. I was overwhelmed but held back my tears. She was saying goodbye with a sign that she knew I'd understand. Today, over 20 years later, I still have not smelled that scent on anyone else. The pain of her loss never went away, but the love she showered during her life and on that day still gives me strength. The mystery of the moment gave me hope to carry on. I feel that she wanted to ease my agony and show me that nothing, not even death, could ever *separate* us.

I had completely forgotten about this extraordinary incident. I knew that Dorna (my cousin) was collecting stories; when I was last in London, we had all gathered over lunch when another cousin shared her story ('Public Phone') with us. During our many phone conversations, Dorna shared more experiences she was including in her book, but none jogged my memory. Until one weekend, after spending three days crying over my son's difficult illness, he got better and I felt a deep release of tension. It was then that the floodgates of my memory opened and I remembered the incident of 2001 in all its glory. I felt shivers down my spine as I was once again in my grandmother's presence. I felt centred and peaceful, knowing she was reminding me that she is always with me, especially during challenging times. I won't forget this powerful event ever again; it is far too precious and invaluable to let it fade into the background of my life.

Emerald

I had recently discovered Christiane Singer, a French author, who in my eyes is a true mystic. I watched her talk on YouTube and was mesmerised by her ability to effortlessly transmit the love and joy of being 'alive'. I enjoyed listening to her so much that I bought three of her books straight away, including one she wrote during the last six months of her life while struggling with cancer. In a nutshell, she inspired me.

She reminded me how very often, despite my best intentions, I go through my day-to-day tasks on autopilot. My to-do list takes all my attention and I take no notice of the 'space' in which I do what I do. In that mode, focused only on the end goal, I let my senses go numb and dim my inner aliveness. Christiane's life and her work are an invitation to feel the vibration of life and become present to the mystery that surrounds us.

On that particular morning, I read a line from one of her books:

'Love like an emerald is green.'

I was captivated by this simple yet profound message, to the point that I put the book down and contemplated its meaning for a few minutes. Throughout the day, these words kept coming to me. 'Love like an emerald is green,' and each time, my heart smiled! This message became my mantra for the entire day, nudging me back to presence and the immediacy of the moment.

In the evening, I visited a friend who has exquisite taste and a talent for making every room buzz with beauty. I probably go to her place no more than once a year. We are close in heart but don't often socialise. When I went to her bathroom, I couldn't believe my eyes. On the shelf, she had three small ornaments, one of them was a green emerald like gemstone, the size of half a palm, resting on a small stand. Had I not been repeating my emerald mantra all day, I would not have felt the joy and excitement that I did at the time. The synchronicity evoked a strong feeling of connection and reassurance which was priceless! It was as if the message of my mantra was being reaffirmed and its truth validated by this timely tiny decoration.

Years later, my friend, who knew how much joy seeing that emerald had brought me, gave it to me as a gift. It now sits on the window shelf, reminding me every day to '*love like an emerald is green*.'

Magnolia Messenger

We had planted a magnolia tree in the front of our house a few years earlier, in the hope that it would brighten our entrance. For some strange reason, it hadn't flowered. We spent hours researching and tending to it but, despite all our tricks to help it blossom, it never did throughout those years.

When my beloved father, who had spent his final years living next door to us passed away, our world lost its colour. Still, in the middle of all that sadness, we found comfort and strength in a place we never expected. When we came back home heavy-hearted after the funeral, we were surprised and touched to find the most beautiful, exceptionally big magnolia flower on our barren tree.

In its simplicity, it quietly invited us to see the light despite our loss. Through its timely appearance we were reminded of the constant flow of birth, death, loss and becoming. What a gift it was to regain clarity and see the miracle of life, of existence, even amidst our deepest grief. On such a difficult day, this flower felt like a messenger from the universe helping us accept that out of nothingness, something sprouts into being and another disappears into it.

What is truly mysterious about this flower is that it is the only flower our tree ever bore on its branches. To this day (some 20 years later), it has never flowered again.

You're a Good Girl

I dreamt of my older cousin who passed away a few years ago. In the dream, he looked at me intently and said something he'd never said before: 'You're a very good girl, do you know that?' I recall feeling so happy to hear him utter the words and when I woke, I was glowing with self assurance. A couple of days later, I called his brother to wish him happy birthday. We talked for a while and after a few minutes, he paused and with the same tone I had heard his brother use in my dream, he said: 'You're a very good girl, do you know that?' I had goosebumps all over. None of them had ever spoken to me like that and now both brothers, one deceased, one on the end of the line said the same words in exactly the same way.

Why did this happen? How did it happen? Was it totally accidental? Was it meant to boost my confidence and affirm that I was on the right path? Whatever it was, it filled me with awe and profound gratitude for how that sweet message came to me – twice in one week.

Maybe I am a good girl, after all!

B for Baba

My partner and I were in the New Forest (UK) in October, enjoying a much-needed rest. In the previous months, we had moved, sold my flat and were in the process of selling his flat in order to buy a house together. This was all physically, emotionally and mentally taxing, which made our mini-break all the more appreciated.

Back in July, after months of searching online for houses and visiting about a dozen properties, we had fallen in love with a beautiful flat with high ceilings and a communal garden. Unfortunately, our offer on it was rejected and we found ourselves back to square one. It was time to reconsider our budget as we were beginning to doubt if it was realistic for what we were looking for. Following a conversation with our mortgage advisor we decided to increase it but this didn't, by any means, resolve our dilemma.

Our first challenge was to do with the number of years left on my partner's flat's lease. This was not an ideal scenario, as the flat had little value with such a short lease. We had to find a buyer willing to purchase it while the lease was being extended. Many were hesitant, as the process to buy while extending was a complicated one. At the same time, we needed at least one offer on this flat before a seller could accept our commitment to buy their property. It was understandably less appealing for sellers on a tight timeline to accept our offer. So even with a larger budget, finding a place that truly felt like home proved difficult.

We were adamant about keeping our spirits high. We kept telling ourselves: 'what is meant for us won't pass us by,' but we still had moments of doubt. Despite our resolve and trust in our vision, there were times when we questioned the feasibility of it all.

Then, we found a house that ticked all of our boxes. It had absolutely everything that we had visualised and more. It was almost too good to be true. The location, the natural surroundings, the relative calm, the house itself, were all just perfect. Although slightly above our already increased budget, it was still within our means. We offered the asking price, knowing that the seller had previously reduced the price twice over the last 12 months. He accepted the offer but gave us a two-month deadline to secure an offer on our flat. The pressure was on!

We really wanted this house.

Following all the great advice we were given by friends and family, we made a few improvements to our flat to make it more appealing to potential buyers. We simplified the decor to make it more neutral and changed our estate agent.

Fast forward to October, during our break in the New Forest, we received some excellent news. Our agent called us to say that we had an enthusiastic buyer, willing to extend the lease while buying the flat. We were over the moon and immediately contacted the agent for the house we hoped to buy. We gave him our good news and agreed to wait for his call the next day, once he spoke to the seller.

The entire evening was spent dreaming and imagining our future. We saw ourselves in our new home and even planned our ideal moving time. We could hardly believe that this was finally happening after months of hard work.

The next day after breakfast, we received a series of blows: first, our buyer wanted to reduce the asking price; with no other choice, we reluctantly agreed. Soon after, the seller's agent informed us that another couple, who had seen the house months before us, had made a very attractive offer in line with its previous price. There was no way we could compete with them; the offer was higher and they were not in any chain. Naturally, the seller had accepted their offer and just like that, we lost our ideal home. Still in shock from this news, we had the third blow: the buyer for our flat pulled out! In 24 hours, everything went sideways.

Needless to say, we were deflated, but we knew better than to fall into the pit of despair. We consoled ourselves with the thought: 'If it wasn't happening, it was for a good reason.' So, to bring our spirits back to light, we decided to go by the sea and let the waves wash over our resistance. Although it was a grey day, breathing the fresh air and witnessing the majesty of the sea brought us to the present moment.

We were each in our little world, letting nature do its magic. As I walked, I could hear the shells and stones beneath my feet. The beauty of the horizon and the sounds of the waves were a perfect background for a heartfelt conversation with Sai Baba (my partner's guru). I call him his guru as I don't subscribe to the disciple/guru relationship and yet, in times of need and difficulties, whenever I felt his presence, it was often followed by either good news or a sense of peace and reassurance. 'Baba' – which means father in my language – I said, 'if you are looking out for us in finding and buying the house of our dreams, give me a sign.' The letter B for Baba on a stone could be a good one, I thought. Years ago, on a holiday, I had looked for and found many stones on a beach with what resembled alphabetical letters on them. Having found the process very relaxing, I decided to meditatively look at the stones under my feet, in case one with the letter B jumped out at me.

After a few minutes, my partner called me, 'Come, have a look at this.' He held up a broken shell moulded into a shape by the waves. He wanted to show me its resemblance to a human heart. When he showed it to me, I saw what it was straight away. I turned it around and there it was: the letter B. I was chuffed! 'You got it, you got the sign.' He looked at me intrigued. 'There is no need for the slightest bit of disappointment. Baba is working on it.' I said with deep conviction, then explained why.

We didn't know at the time, but it turned out we really did have nothing to be sad about. Three months after this incident, we were contacted by the same seller's agent who wanted to know if we were still interested in that property. The intended buyers had been unable to secure their mortgage after all and we were back on track. With a twist of fate, we did finally buy our dream house.

I have kept the shell as a reminder never to lose faith when I feel challenged or disappointed. Every time I look at it I know that I must carry on with a strong heart and sure steps, always.

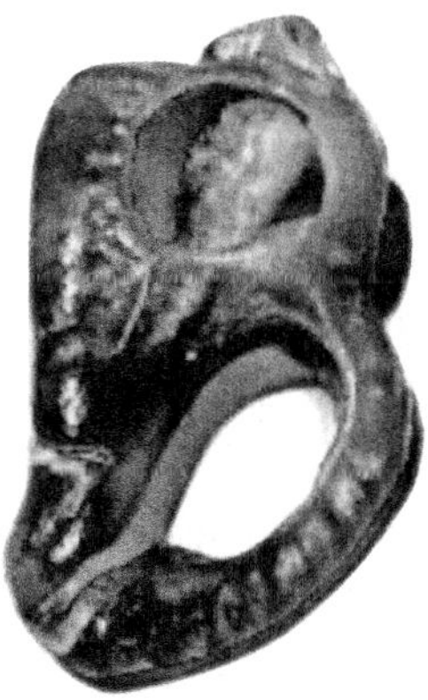

A Selfie or a Sign?

I have a fairly small family on my mum's side, my grandparents and one uncle. On the other hand, I have been lucky to meet her extended family during my visits to Iran: her uncles and aunties and even her grandparents. One uncle – her father's brother – to whom she was very close, was a real character! He was super laid back, always making jokes and had a hearty laugh. He had an eccentric sense of fashion and was clearly a free spirit with artistic tendencies. I would say that it was obvious that having fun, staying light and bright, was his priority in life. Relatively speaking, I spent more time with him than anyone else in my mother's extended family, even more than I did with my grandfather. Her uncle was open to adventure so, during one of our visits, he volunteered to take us on a day trip. We explored Noush-Abad, an underground city that is believed to be 1500 years old. We also spent another mini-holiday together in Marseille, where he used to live and where my mum grew up. He had gone to visit and invited us to join him. Although I don't have many memories as we only met a handful of times, I have a clear image of him – always wearing his bucket hat, large glasses, his thick grey beard and a big smile.

One morning in April 2024, I woke up to missed calls from my mum, so I called her back. From the way she spoke, I knew she had bad news to share. My stomach clenched in anticipation. The only thought that crossed my mind was 'Someone has died'.
I was right. Her uncle had unexpectedly passed away the day before, at the age of 72. Even though she was informed immediately, she had delayed giving me the news. When I heard of his passing, my heart sank – not just because he was gone, but because what I experienced the evening before took on a very different meaning. My feelings of sadness and shock were mixed with a sense of wonder as I realised that what had happened may not have been a mere coincidence.

Initially, I couldn't express my sadness; it was all too much to process.

The first thing I said was 'Oh my god, you won't believe what happened yesterday!' and asked her to check her phone as I was sending her a selfie.

The night before I was in a local club in Ibiza where I live, to see my favourite Dj when a man caught my eye. He was standing on the stairs with a bucket hat, large glasses and a big grey beard. His energy was very familiar and I just couldn't help but see my mum's uncle in him. Although he was younger, the resemblance was unbelievable. I pointed him out to my friend and said, 'I just have to get a photo with him to show my mum.' It wasn't until the second time that I saw him in the evening, that I gathered the courage to approach him. I went up to him and asked him for a selfie, explaining that I couldn't get over how much he looked like my great uncle. He happily obliged. We had a little chat and he even told me that he likes the men in San Remo, which made me chuckle, as I recently had a little romance with a man from San Remo myself. We parted. I danced the night away and I forgot all about my little encounter and my great uncle.

Now, my mother was telling me that he was gone.

After hearing the story of my previous night and seeing the photo, I sensed her smile. I could guess what she was thinking and felt her pain transform into wonder. 'Let's wait and see if he will give us a sign', is what she had told her brother the day before. We both agreed that whether this was a sign from the beyond or not, it was indeed too much of a coincidence to dismiss.

I still cannot get over the fact that I had never seen this man before, even though we both regularly go to the same and only club that is open in the winter. It's even stranger that despite visiting his workplace a few times since meeting him months ago, I haven't seen him again! I am left in awe that the only time I met him was on the very night of the day that my great uncle had passed away. It certainly feels as though he had found a way to come and say goodbye.

The Palace of Dreams

When I was a little girl, around six or seven, I had a recurring dream of a grand marble and gold palace with striking red stairs. From the outside, it looked like an ordinary grey townhouse, but when I went inside with my parents, it would transform into a magical place where I felt free to run upstairs and play. In the dreams, I felt at home and at ease and each time, I was filled with immense joy and peace.

Fast forward several years, when I was 19, I worked in Waitrose supermarket during my gap year before university. One day, a man came in and started asking me lots of questions: 'Oh, you're very young; are you a student?' I said, 'Yes, I've received an offer from Durham and will be starting my BA in PPE (Philosophy, Politics and Economics) from September.' Out of the blue, he said, 'Oh, you should work for the Foreign Office.' I didn't know anything about that, so I asked him to tell me more. He suggested I look it up and check out the internship and graduate schemes that they offer. He passionately encouraged me to explore their opportunities to the point that he ended up chasing me around the shop, convincing me to apply and work for them. He even said that I should be a diplomat! Personally, I think he really wanted the Foreign Office to become more diverse, as I am originally from Barbados and he was Jamaican. The entire conversation was so unusual and random that it triggered my curiosity so when I went home, I Googled it. Lo and behold, the Foreign Office building was exactly the same as my childhood's recurring dream, which I had named 'the palace of dreams'. It was exactly – just exactly – the same. The layout of the stairs, the gold, the marble. Even the exterior was the same. It was a spooky experience that left me both shocked and intrigued.

I decided to attend their annual open day. This happens in September during Open House London – an architecture festival that celebrates London's architectural heritage. It is the only time during the year that they open to the public for a weekend, allowing Londoners and tourists to explore the famous interior. The experience was surreal – the street, the atmosphere; everything felt just like in my childhood dreams.

A few years later, as I was completing my degree, I applied for a summer internship in the civil service, a post open to both finalists (those completing their last year of undergraduate study) and those completing their penultimate year. I applied as a finalist and fortunately was offered a place. The offer came just before I graduated and I was to find out which department I'd been posted to soon after. I could have been posted anywhere, but as fate would have it, I was posted to the Foreign Office. This was an unlikely outcome as the odds were slim and the competition high. As if being surprised once wasn't enough, a couple of years later, as part of my graduate scheme, I was assigned to the Foreign Office again. I was told how impossible it was for anyone on the graduate scheme to be posted there, as the Foreign Office traditionally did not take generalists. It felt like a twist of fate to be welcomed by the Foreign Office not once, but twice in such an unprecedented way.

Right from the start, the coincidences around this gripped me. When I initially Googled it, I saw the image and the first thing that came to my mind was, 'This is 'the palace of dreams." What also came up in the search was a BBC documentary about the Foreign Office. What do you think the title of this documentary was? It was called The Palace of Dreams, which you can find on YouTube.

How could that be possible? I even thought I might have seen this documentary on television when I was a child, but as it was only aired in 2010, that wasn't the answer. By then, I was a teenager and had already named my dreams. Was it a premonition? I cannot brush it off as mere coincidence, yet I can't find the meaning behind it. I'm simply amazed that a complete stranger would lead me to discover and ultimately play a part in 'The Palace of *my* Dreams'.

It is through experiences such as this that I marvel at the amazing way life has of paving the way for the most unexpected journeys.

Heavenly Swirling Notes

We went on holiday to Gran Canaria, just a few months after my husband, Michael, lost his mother. She was from Greece, full of sunshine and energy and would never miss an opportunity to dance. She loved music!

On this particular trip, we had no specific plans to visit anywhere special. We went there only to rest our minds and heal our grieving hearts. One morning, we decided to take a leisurely walk. After a few hours of wandering around, admiring the natural surroundings, collecting souvenirs and visiting a local café, we still weren't ready to go back to the hotel. So, we thought it would be a good idea to catch a bus and go to a nearby little town. When we arrived at the bus station, we realised that we had just missed the last bus going that way. This meant we had to walk a pretty long way to reach the town.

We strolled around, not really knowing if the paths we were taking would lead us to where we wanted. Eventually, after some meandering, we found ourselves in the right town, standing in a quaint little square. Right in front of us, there were three people playing music: two young men and a girl who stood between them. It turned out they were just about to play their final piece.

To our astonishment, this last song happened to be the favourite piece of Michael's late mother. It was a song we had only ever heard in Greece – an old-fashioned, almost forgotten piece, rarely played and unknown to most. Needless to say, the coincidence was quite moving, given that he had only lost his mother a few months before.

I will never forget the profound connection and the powerful emotions that washed over us the moment the music began. For Michael especially, the fact that this uncommon song, was being played in a small, remote town outside of Greece, was very soothing. It brought him a deep sense of comfort and acceptance.

After playing and moving us to our core, the musicians ended their performance and began packing up their instruments.

Reflecting on it all, we saw all the little twists of fate that brought us to experience this beautiful, unique and unforgettable moment. Had we not missed the bus, taken a different path or arrived a few minutes later or earlier, we might have simply walked through the square and missed this special moment. It felt as though life had orchestrated our choices, leading us to be in the right place at the right time to hear the right music.

We were in awe of the serendipity that had brought us to a place which was momentarily filled with his mum's presence as the notes of her favourite music swirled around the square.

Duck and Potato Dauphinoise

One afternoon, sitting at home, I suddenly had this really really strong craving. I fancied this very specific meal: a duck à l'orange with potato dauphinoise. My mouth watered as I visualised every detail of this plate.

This particular dish is quite rare on most menus and is impossible to find in local restaurants. It was indeed a very random request from my taste buds or shall I say my guts! I couldn't explain my sudden desire for this meal. I had only ever heard of pregnant women having such strong and specific cravings but this wasn't my case. There was no duck à l'orange with potato dauphinoise anywhere near and I wasn't going to make one so, that was that. I lingered in the fantasy, savouring it in my imagination, before simply carrying on with my day!

About a week later, on the weekend, I decided to take a trip to my favourite museum, the V&A in London. As a member, I headed to their members' room to have a bite. On the menu, lo and behold I read: Duck à l'orange with potato dauphinoise. Needless to say, as expected, I thoroughly enjoyed it. For the most important part because my wish had come true. It was as if I had placed a cosmic order from the divine menu and it was brought to me in style, on a plate in my favourite place. The fact that it took the universal chef one week to prepare it, was of no concern at all!

Admittedly, I was also spooked. It was the precision, the fact that this dish was exactly what I had visualised and almost tasted. It was as if a picture was taken from my inner world and projected out there a week later. Seeing my imagination and reality intertwining in this way was a magical gift that I treasure to this day.

Finding Humanity

Every day, on my way back from work, I used to pass our local supermarket. Naturally, I became a frequent shopper for many years – nearly 20 to be precise – and got to know the members of the staff very well. Their customer service has a great reputation, with most staff being polite and very helpful. Shopping there is – in general – a delightful experience.

Having shared this story with many, I've realised that I am not alone in gravitating toward the checkout with the shortest queue or the friendliest member of staff. In this branch, there was a cashier who was very serious; he never smiled and as if forced, he'd mumble a hello back to me whenever I went to him to pay for my items. I often felt that he didn't have the right personality for a job that required a lot of human interactions.

Over the years, I applied many tactics to get him to open up. It seemed to me that he was wrapped up in his own cocoon unwilling to come out. Eventually, after I realised that my efforts to build a human connection had no effect, I gave up trying. I began to avoid him having finally realised I wasn't keen to be served by someone I perceived as a robot. I later found out that many locals had the same experience with him and would also stay away from him when possible.

Throughout my adult life, I have often pondered why these small things matter to me so much. Why did I feel uncomfortable standing there in the absence of connection, recognition or interaction? Why couldn't I just ignore it or be okay with it? Finally, I concluded that the reason 'robotic' people sparked a sense of unease in me was because of my desire for them to change. I wanted them to come to life, to engage and be present. When they didn't, I mirrored what I perceived as their disconnection and ended up disconnecting from myself.

This was uncomfortable and I needed to change. I needed to practice reconnecting with myself when I felt the lack of interaction and engagement in such cases. In order to stay centred and in the flow of the moment when faced with such people, I started bringing my attention back to my senses and my own internal energy. I wanted to learn to respect their choices in how they turned up in the world and drop my own conflicting attitude towards their way of being.

Although I still need to catch myself when I recognise that I have fallen into old habits, what happened on this specific day was a true turning point:

I was choosing which cashier to go to and saw him but turned my eyes away, naturally avoiding him. It dawned on me that I was still stuck in my old behavioural patterns, but as I was determined to break old emotional habits, I decided to approach him and put an end to my discomfort.

I wasn't going to try to change him or attempt to connect. My sole intention was to stay centred within myself. Instead of blaming his attitude for my lack of ease, I focused on the physical sensations of unease in my own body. I noticed my breath was shallow and my belly was tense. I released that tension and let go of any other tightness that was blocking my breath. I relaxed my jaw, softened my neck and shoulders and slowly but surely, I started feeling great. I became fully present to the orchestra of sounds made by the tills and the entire scene came to life. I had completely forgotten about the cashier. I was content and comfortable in my own skin.

Suddenly, this man, who had hardly looked at or spoken to me before, picked my rhubarb bag from the conveyor belt and with a big smile, said: 'What do you cook with these? My wife makes the best dessert with them.' I nearly collapsed! He talked, he smiled and he enjoyed his wife's desserts. He was human after all!

I was overjoyed, not because he had connected but because *the timing* gave me a profound insight. It was only when I let go of my agenda and freed my breath and body from tension that he was able to relax and connect. He became his comfortable self only when he stopped feeling the unconscious pressure that I was putting on us both. My difficulty in standing there had more to do with my inability to breathe well – in his 'serious' presence – than his behaviour.

In that moment, my teachers' message became clear:
'Change yourself and the world will change in front of your eyes.'
This, I was shown, in the most unmistakable and obvious way.

Since then, we have no trouble connecting. There is no avoiding, no discomfort and we are on friendly terms. Who would have thought? Humanity, connection and the ability to breathe do seem to go hand in hand!

For Now I am Home

It was a hot, balmy day in 2021. I was travelling on the tube back from work and the train was slowly crawling along in staccato style to each stop. Eventually, it came to a complete halt for 15 minutes, leaving me no choice but to exit and look for a different way home. I was in a strange space within myself.

Having experienced many disappointments in relationships, I had come to accept that being single might be my destiny. Yet, occasionally, a pang of longing would take hold of me, as if something essential was missing. In the past week, every time I meditated, I would see a fleeting image of a man flickering in front of me. I would get a glimpse of his brown eyes, curly hair and strong arms but the image would disappear very soon afterwards.

As I went up the hill in Highgate (London) on this typical summer's day to take a bus, the sunlight on parasols and sounds of laughter from a nearby pub caught my attention. As I passed 'The Woodman,' a thought crossed my mind: 'Wouldn't it be nice to be on a date in this garden pub right now...' At that moment, out of the blue, the familiar pang hit me again.

Eventually, I arrived home, feeling hot and bothered, wanting nothing more than to isolate myself from the world. In a state of slight gloom and self-pity, I decided to delete a dating app that had been on my phone for months. I hadn't bothered to look at it for a while. Before deleting it I opened it and to my surprise, there was a message waiting for me. In my dating app profile, I had intentionally included an excessive amount of cat talk, knowing only a man who would embrace the crazy teacher-cat-lady cliché would be worth my time. His first question was about cats and although I couldn't decipher how he really looked from his photographs, I decided to throw caution to the wind and replied.

We carried on communicating for about a week, laughing and bantering with ease. Soon after, he asked me out on a date. I was both thrilled and slightly stunned when he suggested 'The Woodman.' The same pub where the pang had hit me and I wished to be there with someone special. Coincidentally, he lived just around the corner and had been going there a fair bit recently. The thought briefly crossed my mind about whether he might have been there that evening when I passed it after school. Maybe his laughter was one I had heard but I quickly brushed it off, not wanting to make him or the incident too significant in my head.

When we met, there was a strange sense of familiarity, but I wasn't entirely sure how I felt about him or even why I felt that way. It wasn't until our third date that I realised he was the man I had been seeing in my visions and meditations. As we got to know each other better, we discovered how surprisingly similar our life paths had been at different points. We were going to the same places as teenagers during the same years and he had worked across from where I lived for years. We both found it astonishing that we even shared Scottish Italian heritage with grandparents from the same region in Italy. Gradually, our connection deepened and we fell in love in a way that neither of us had experienced before. Though our parents had always said we would know when it happened, neither of us had truly believed them.

For our first holiday, we decided to travel to Italy, to Naples and a village outside it, then to Rome to follow in the footsteps of our ancestors. It was an unforgettable experience and our love grew stronger. Perhaps powered by the awe-inspiring presence of Mount Vesuvius or the strange feeling of being at home on those grounds.

When we returned from our holiday, I noticed a postcard on my doorstep showing an image of an ancient obelisk against a cobalt blue, cloudless sky. The first line read: 'Behold these ancient symbols of power!' To my surprise, the postcard was from a couple who, to my knowledge, had divorced. Intrigued, I texted my friend to find out if they had reconciled. She told me that they had actually sent the postcard from Ethiopia seven years ago, but it had only just arrived. I found out that the image on the postcard was an obelisk in the ancient city of Aksum, one of eight that remained. Interestingly, in the 1930s, this particular obelisk had been taken from Ethiopia, cut up and transported to Italy, first to Naples and then to Rome - the very journey we had just taken. Eventually, it was repatriated and became a symbol of unity and renewed friendship between the two lands.

We recently celebrated our first year together and we continue to experience moments of minute synchronicity regularly - saying words at the same time, having the same names for our imagined children and feeling a general sense of ease and 'luckiness' when we are together. We have planned many more trips and even a not-so-secret runaway wedding. Of course, we are not naive and know that we will be facing adversities along the way. But, much like the obelisk, I have weathered many journeys and come close to being broken but for now, I am home.

My Birth

My mother tells this story:
My parents were sent from Iran to France to further their education. Both their fathers, who had known each other at university, sent their children to Besançon. This is how they met and fell in love. Soon after, they decided to get married, but had to overcome the hurdle of convincing their parents. Initially, there was a lot of resistance since they were both in their early 20s and the original plan behind sending them abroad was for them to study, not to start a family! Finally, they managed to persuade them and the wedding took place in the summer of 1968, just in time for them to return to France and start the new term in Paris.

When I was conceived, it came as a bit of a surprise. From the many stories I've heard, it seems I was very eager to land on this planet!

One evening, when my mother was eight months pregnant, my grandmother – Maman Batoul – suddenly became convinced that her daughter was in labour. Overwhelmed, she went up on the balcony, trying to hold her tears back. She didn't know what to do with the many emotions she was feeling; worry, anticipation and joy made her pace the room, unable to keep still. She couldn't sleep the entire night and pleaded with my grandfather to book her a flight, insisting that she knew I was being born.

His logical mind couldn't accept it, of course, as it was a whole month before the due date. Naturally, he tried to calm her down and bring some rationality to her seemingly irrational behaviour. In those days, there were no immediate means of communication like phones, FaceTime, or WhatsApp. The only way to communicate was through snail mail or, in emergencies, telegraphs, which could take a few hours to arrive.

My grandmother had no way to confirm her 'knowing,' but her restlessness finally convinced my grandfather to book her a flight to Paris.

The following day a telegraph arrived confirming that I had landed on this physical plane. By then she was already set and ready to go. All she needed to do was pack her bags, relieved and happy to know that her instincts had been right all along.

There is something that makes loved ones sense what is happening to the other even across different continents. Is it telepathy? The emotional bond? Love? Whatever it is, there are far too many similar stories pointing to something beyond the physical that makes this kind of communication possible. I for one, believe that science will one day uncover the reasons behind what feel like a mystery today.

Manifesting

For the past few years, my husband and I had been struggling financially. For reasons we couldn't fathom, none of us was getting as much work as we were used to. We were scraping by to make ends meet, which was completely unlike what we were used to. We went through dark moments that I don't wish to relive and yet, strangely enough, I wouldn't have wanted to miss the opportunity to grow either. It is true what Rumi says:
'The wound is the place where the Light enters you.'

Through our unexpected challenges, we learned that we never had control over the results of our actions, even though it surely felt that we did. We worked hard and enjoyed the fruits of our actions, which gave us the illusion that it was our doing that affected the outcome. So when, regardless of how hard we tried, all our attempts to earn a living failed, we realised how oblivious we'd been to the truth. Today, we do what we do, working towards our goal, knowing the result is indeed out of our control. Our struggles also reminded us that the things that truly made us happy had no financial value. They were priceless and no buying power could ever bring them to our lives.

I was proud to discover that our previous financial success had not tied me to my material belongings. Though I have a taste for luxury, I saw how easy it was for me to let go of my possessions. Just as I had hoped, none of my belongings ever owned me; I owned them and I gave them up without hesitation when needed.

For a while, we did hold on to two flats as an integral part of our pension plan. However, we soon realised that the possibility of a financial turnaround in the near future was very dim and we had no choice but to put them up for sale. Alas, no one showed any interest. When eventually the tenants who no longer felt settled left, we couldn't take on new ones knowing how quickly we were prepared to sell. This meant that in our dire financial situation, we were also unable to collect our usual rental income. Months passed and nothing changed despite reducing the sale price to the limit of what was financially feasible.

To keep my head above water and not drown in huge emotional waves, I resorted to all the techniques known to human kind. Meditation became my lifeline; it kept me sane and able to carry on without losing my mind. One day, quite accidentally, I came across an audiobook by Wayne Dyer called 'Meditations for Manifesting'. I had always been a big fan of Wayne as listening to him had a centring effect on me. The name of this audiobook was appealing; I needed to meditate and I definitely needed to manifest money, or we would soon lose the roof over our heads. I listened with urgency, drinking in every word, then sat to meditate to 'manifest'. The ancient technique was simple: I was to vocalise the sound of Aaah comfortably for 20 minutes, sending the sounds up to the centre of my head. I was to recall my intention every now and again as I chanted. I followed the instruction to the letter and once I finished, I felt livelier, filled with joy and hope. It was hard to believe, but the magic of the meditation, showed itself within minutes. After a month of no work, I received a phone call from a client wanting to book a few sessions with me. I was buzzing with excitement and shared what happened with my husband. I told him that he had to try, even if he didn't believe in it. His response was unlike his usual self; desperation had changed the man and he was open to trying anything. So, the next morning, eager to manifest a magical solution to our predicament, we both sat and chanted Aaah for 20 minutes.

Minutes after our chant and I am not exaggerating, our estate agent called my husband with unexpected news. He had met a couple of students who showed interest in one of the flats – not to buy, but to rent. They knew that the flat was up for sale but still wanted to live there and were willing to pay six months in advance. Not only that, the same flat had a potential buyer who was happy to wait for the completion to take place in six months. We thought this was too good to be true, but within three days, the money was in our account and we were, for a while, given the chance to breathe again.

Was it really the power of our chanting meditation that threw the dice in our favour? Was our intention that powerful? My Buddhist friends would definitely agree. They see this kind of magic all the time. But for me, this was no usual affair. All I knew was that whatever made the events turn to our advantage could not be explained with our rational mind.

We are indeed unknown to ourselves and unfamiliar with the power that resides in us all.
To this power, I bow, each and every day.

White Dove

In December 2020, I was fighting a difficult case of Covid-19 for nearly a month, but I wasn't getting any better. The symptoms were getting worse until one day, we had no choice but to call an ambulance. Due to the pressure on the National Health Service, I was advised to stay home if I could. I was well aware that the situation in hospitals was critical. They were overwhelmed with severe cases of Covid-19 and I knew that those were the ones they had to prioritise. So, I stayed at home despite the fact that, with each day passing, I was losing more strength. I was becoming more and more frail and fragile, to the point that I could barely walk. There were nights when I doubted if I'd wake up in the morning. My lungs were in no great condition and breathing was no longer something that I could take for granted. My family was aware of how weak I'd become but we all agreed that it was best not to go to hospital. We all hoped that as a big strong man, with lungs twice as big as the average person, I would be able to pull through. I made very little fuss and waited for my immune system to work its magic.

Alas, my condition worsened on Christmas Eve after hearing that my brother-in-law, my wife's brother, had suddenly died of a heart attack. We couldn't believe it! He was a fit man in his 50s, same age as me, with no sign of any heart condition.

As heart issues are often hereditary, a family friend suggested that my wife get her heart checked. Following on the advice, she scheduled a checkup at a local private hospital, where they offered CT scans at a walk-in clinic. Luckily, she suggested that I'd go with her, hoping they could also scan my lungs. As soon as we arrived at the clinic, they ran some tests. The specialist, who hadn't yet seen me, while examining my scan, had assumed that I was already in a coma. She was shocked to hear that I had walked into the clinic myself as the scan had revealed that 60% of my lungs were damaged. I was immediately rushed to the intensive care unit.

Initially, some of the medications seemed to have positive effects, but my condition deteriorated until I slipped into unconsciousness. It was impossible for them to put me on a ventilator. Instead, I later found out, they used a sophisticated but invasive machine to oxygenate my body and remove carbon dioxide. Had it not been for that procedure, I might not be here today to tell the tale.

I regained consciousness three days later, but my condition had worsened. A normal oxygen level is 93 to 100% and 88% requires (urgent) medical attention. My oxygen levels had by then plummeted down to 58% and breathing was a severe struggle. The medical team were doing everything they could to improve my condition. Although risky, they didn't have a choice but to give me a cocktail of experimental drugs as I was not responding to conventional treatments. I couldn't ignore the worried faces of the medical team so I knew that things were grim.

One afternoon, it became clear to me that I was dying. They transferred me to a special room where three other Covid-19 patients were suffering. They placed two fans near me to cool my body down from an intense fever and insisted that I don't let nurses from the next shift move them away. I noticed a fellow patient in agony, crying out that he was burning from inside and could no longer take the heat. I asked a nurse to give him one of the fans, but she refused, explaining that my condition was far worse. His extreme emotional response was apparently a common symptom of Covid-19. I suggested opening the windows, but I was told it was impossible. They explained to me that these were glass walls and there was no way of opening them. Drawing up from my experience in construction, I knew they were mistaken. I had overseen the building of many hospitals so managed to convince them to take me near the window. I needed to find the security button that would slide the window open. To their delight and surprise, I managed to open one of them and bring some much-needed relief from our intense fever.

Shortly after, a porter took me downstairs for an MRI scan. I could feel myself slipping into unconsciousness again. The young man doing the MRI was exceptionally kind and compassionate. He must have seen something concerning on the scan, for despite my condition, he gave me a heartfelt hug when we finished the procedure. I took it as a clear sign that he believed my time was up.

Back in my room, the head nurse came to me and held my hand. She had tears in her eyes. She was looking at a dying man, I could sense it. I assumed that the doctor had informed her that my chances of surviving that evening were slim. The scan had showed that my entire body was riddled with blood clots and I could see that my systolic blood pressure had soared to 250. Unable to hold her tears back she said: 'Don't worry, we are with you and will take good care of you'. The window was still open and I felt the cool air as I found myself disappearing into the void.

Just at that moment, a woman whom I had previously given Reiki energy healing to during her battle with pancreatic cancer, called me. She had become a firm believer in energy healing and was convinced that our sessions had contributed greatly to her recovery. Though unable to speak, I could hear her clearly and understand her pleas. In between her sobs, she managed to suggest that I give myself energy healing, as she had read that it was potentially as effective as receiving it from others. I knew that too but, the idea hadn't even crossed my mind. I had no life left in me and energy healing did take its toll on me. I didn't believe I had what it took to do it but I had nothing to lose as I was rapidly slipping away from life. So, I placed my hands on my chest and to my surprise, my fingers grew stiff and warm. Typically, this was a clear sign that energy was flowing and healing was taking place. I can't recall how long I practiced self-healing, two minutes, five minutes or more. It all seems like a blur. As I was doing it though, I lost consciousness. It must have been around 11 pm.

My next recollection was waking up at 5:15 am on January 8th. I had nothing on; no clothes, no machines attached and the IV drips had been removed. Even the oxygen supply machine had been turned off. I was aware that I was moving with an ease that I hadn't felt in weeks. When I saw the wet floor and the bruises on my chest and belly, I knew what had happened. It all looked too familiar as I had seen my father after they had resuscitated him. I knew they must have done the same on me. I noticed a shadow behind the glass curtain and cried out, 'sister'. She screamed and rushed towards the doctors. Only earlier, they had spent half an hour trying to revive me after a full cardiac arrest and had declared me dead when their efforts failed. I later learnt that I was to be taken to the mortuary when it opened at 7 am. But now, I was alive and alert. Everyone hurried back into the room, reconnecting all the machines. My oxygen levels had come back to a healthy 99% and my blood pressure was also completely normal. They rushed me back to the MRI. When the doctor came to show me the result of the MRI, he asked me if I believed in miracles. I told him that I knew anything was possible. He glanced again at the results and in a tone of joyous disbelief told me that there was not a single blood clot in my entire body.

At this point, my wife called me. She immediately became aware of the energy behind my voice, as I sounded a lot more like myself. We were both very emotional and didn't know whether to laugh or cry. I told her what I remembered: When I put my hands on my chest to give myself Reiki, I fell into a dreamlike state with vivid sensations. I felt a white dove on my chest and the sensations of its wings moving rapidly over me. It was as if it had a mission to clean and clear any trace of infection from my lungs. This dove was bringing me back to health. I knew it and I could feel its tiny weight on my chest as it was cleansing my lungs.

I think it is important to say here that my wife and I were talking in Persian so when Trevor, another patient younger than me in his 40s, said what he said when I put the phone down, I couldn't believe my ears. He looked at me, the window, then back at me and said: 'I want what you had'. 'Excuse me?' I replied. He repeated, his voice trembling: 'I want what you had, I want your white dove. You were dead and a white dove came in, sat on your chest and brought you back to life.' He couldn't hold back his tears and I was left speechless.

Had he hallucinated? Had we both shared the same hallucination? I would never know. What I know is that the white dove felt real and after being declared dead, I came back to life. Even the staff started calling our ward 'the miracle ward'.

I did eventually give Trevor some healing while the head nurse stood by and watched us. I would never forget her face in that moment. She was glowing, clearly taken by a sense of sacred awe for what we had all witnessed on 8th January 2021.

Through the Forest Have I Gone

I have been living in London for over 35 years. I was born in France and completed all my studies there before I came to London as a young adult. My father is French and my late mother was British. A few years ago, while visiting my father's house in France to celebrate my birthday, something extraordinary happened.

On the day of my birthday, I randomly picked a French book from the hundreds sitting on my father's bookshelves. The book intrigued me and I decided to snuggle up with it on the sofa. It completely captivated me and I ended up reading a few chapters. As much as I wanted to continue reading, I needed a short break, so I put the book down. Realising I didn't have a bookmark, I checked inside the book hoping to find one tucked away. I was delighted when I found a card at the end of the book that could serve as a perfect bookmark.

I took a closer look at it. On the front of the card was a drawing of a scene from Shakespeare's play 'A Midsummer Night's Dream', with a short quote: 'Through the forest have I gone.' I opened the card and to my utter surprise, I read the heartfelt birthday wishes addressed to me, written by my late Aunty Marilyn, my mother's sister.

Discovering this old card, sent by my deceased and beloved aunty years ago, tucked inside a French book that I randomly picked up, on the very day of my birthday, was beyond me. As if that was not enough, this was the aunty for whom I had dedicated a tree – after her passing – through the Woodland Trust. When I read the quote printed on the card, it was as if she had written it from another dimension to say that she was part of the forest, in an attempt to acknowledge how I had expressed my love for her. How could that be though? This was a card she had sent long before I dedicated a tree for her!

The whole experience felt like a magical play of space and time which filled me with an indescribable sense of aliveness. I felt such deep connection with Aunty Marilyn. To find this card, years after she first sent it, on my actual birthday, was indeed a surreal gift.

It is impossible to explain phenomena such as these with our current understanding of time. Perhaps one day, the concept of time will be seen differently and we will have a rational explanation for such events. For now, I am happy to label them as *magical*!

A Bridge by the River

Some years ago, when I was a young adult, I went on holiday to Ireland, staying in hostels, enjoying meeting new people and soaking up the atmosphere and beauty. I made friends with Valerie who was hiking on her own around Ireland and planning to travel to England later. I suggested she could stay with me during her stay in England, as I lived in Oxford, in a house with spare rooms at the time. Although no concrete plan was ever made, I came home from my holiday with a general feeling that she would turn up at some point.

One morning, I got a very strong urge to go for a walk. It was as if an unseen force was moving me. I allowed myself to be pulled in the direction of the river and walked along its banks. I was led on a route I had never taken. 'Why am I going this way?' I wondered. It felt very peculiar to tread on an unfamiliar path for no obvious reason, yet I trusted my instincts. Despite moments of boredom and uncertainty, I continued until I came to a bridge, where the road crossed the river. This 'pull' took me up onto the road and I stood there, wondering what on earth I was doing standing there – doing nothing. The feeling was alien to me and for a minute, I was a stranger to myself!

But just then, a lorry pulled up on the other side of the road and it became clear to me why I had stood there, waiting. I saw Valerie waving to me from the window. She jumped out of the lorry and was surprised to see me standing by the road as if waiting to greet her. I had no idea that she was on her way to me, yet I stood there as if I had known the exact time that she was going to pass through. I was as amazed as she was. How could I have possibly known? Clearly, something in me did, but it certainly wasn't conscious. It was something beyond thought, which was powerful enough to make us cross paths in the most unusual and wondrous way.

Her arrival couldn't have been more timely. She was a Godsend!

I had been struggling with writing a job application at the time. This kind of thing wasn't my forte, but she was an expert in that area. Having worked in lots of different jobs and being generally more streetwise than me, she was the perfect candidate to give me invaluable advice. We spent a wonderful few days together and I am grateful for her providential arrival. Without her, I doubt that I would have been able to secure the job I was applying for. I was guided to her and she guided me through exactly what I needed at the time.

Since then, I have wondered what it is that inspires us into action. I used to believe it was our mind, but what happened that day showed me that there is more to it. Perhaps our personal mind is connected to a collective mind, allowing us to receive information that are beyond the limits of our own thoughts.

A Sign of Hope

The last seven years have been the toughest chapter of my adult life. I have witnessed so many challenges, have gone through many losses and have needed to adapt to many new and unwelcome circumstances. I long for the day I can look back and think: 'I did it, I stood firm in the face of the storm and became stronger!' I dream of the moment when I say to myself: 'As hard as it was, my spirit was stronger!' Unfortunately, for now, there are many days when I feel drained, uninspired and afraid of what the future may hold. The knot I feel in my stomach, the shooting pain in my back when fear takes hold of me can, at times, feel unbearable. I know that '***this too shall pass***' but this knowledge doesn't always stop me from shaking in my boots.

On that particular day, I had to go out to run an errand. While driving, I found myself overwhelmed with emotions. Tears streamed down my face as I wholeheartedly pleaded for a sign. A sign that would assure me that everything would eventually be alright. A sign that would encourage me to endure the weight of my struggle, just a little longer, until it passed.

All of a sudden, my sobs and desperate calls were interrupted. No words can express the depth and immensity of my joy when my eyes caught sight of a vibrant rainbow – a powerful symbol of hope, resilience and new beginnings. Nature was showing me that storms don't last forever and when they pass, beautiful colours fill the sky. I was elated. I was still. 'Better times are ahead' was the message of this rainbow. I let its beauty wash over me and was filled with a deep sense of calm. Its appearance in that precise moment felt very personal. It was as if it had revealed itself just to lift me from despair into a profound, soul-soothing peace.

Digital Dimension and Beyond

My grandfather, whose name was Fakhruddin and whom I affectionately called Pedar (meaning father), was the fittest man I knew. In his youth, he had won many swimming races and had a big collection of trophies to show for it. He was deeply into Persian martial arts and religiously began his mornings exercising in the garden, regardless of the weather, never missing his routine. Skipping a 100 times and doing headstands were always part of his routine, though he changed other exercises regularly. I remember seeing an impressive photo of him once, holding a man with one straight arm above his head.

We all looked up to him and wished we could be as disciplined as him in all aspects, especially when it came to exercise and fitness. At 85, he had the posture of a 40-year-old and looked healthier and more energetic than his younger siblings. He never suffered from any illness and never needed a doctor until the last two weeks of his life in the hospital. It started with a cold that turned into pneumonia, yet he died peacefully in his sleep in September 2009.

For reasons that escape me, I couldn't fly from London to attend his funeral in Iran. I kept regular contact with my father during that period, hoping to provide some solace despite being so far away. In the evening after his burial, I felt immensely guilty for letting my grandfather down by not being present for the ceremony. With a heavy heart, I apologised to him and wished he'd forgive me. I hadn't yet cried – which is very unlike me – but was overtaken by shame and guilt.

The following day, I turned on my computer to get on with some work. I opened my emails and nearly jumped out of my chair as I read the subject of one email. It read: 'Fakhruddin khan left you a new scrap!'.

I opened the email, practically shaking and read:

'Hi, how r u?'
Fakhruddin is a very uncommon name in my country and as such I knew only one; my grandfather. In Persian, 'khan' is used after a name when addressing a man as a sign of respect. It used to be a title that was reserved for noblemen but is now widely used. Many called my grandfather 'Fakhruddin khan', so to see his name appearing on my screen, the day after his passing, was unexpected and extraordinary. Especially as he had never used a computer or sent me an email while he was alive.

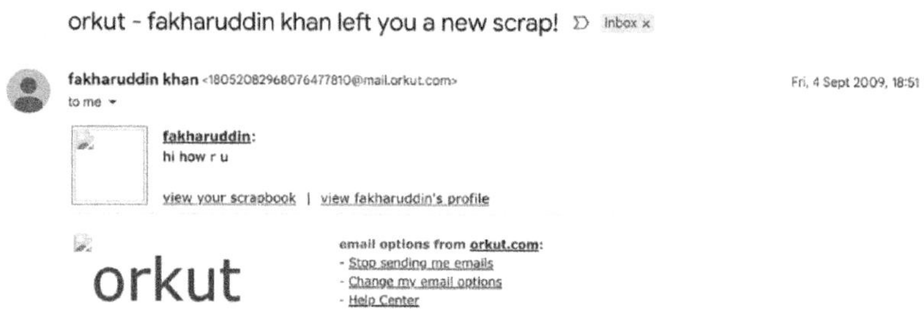
orkut - fakharuddin khan left you a new scrap! Inbox ×

fakharuddin khan <18052082968076477810@mail.orkut.com> Fri, 4 Sept 2009, 18:51
to me

fakharuddin:
hi how r u

view your scrapbook | view fakharuddin's profile

orkut

email options from orkut.com:
- Stop sending me emails
- Change my email options
- Help Center

The shock left me in deep silence at first – just like the one before a storm. Moments later though, I was overwhelmed by a flood of tears and sobbed for what felt like an eternity.

I felt his loving presence. It was as if he was asking me to be at peace with myself and showing me that there were no hard feelings! Even though I cried most of the morning, my tears were more a testament to the love we shared than an expression of my grief.

Later on, when I calmed down, I saw that this email had come from Orkut, one of the early social media platforms before Facebook was a big hit. I had joined Orkut (a popular platform in Eastern countries) at my family's request but had hardly ever used it. It turned out that a Pakistani man I didn't know, called Fakhruddin, wanted to say hi and befriend me.

What are the odds of that? This totally random person, who happened to share the very same name as my grandfather, decided to send me a message the day after his funeral. All he was thinking was broadening his network. He never intended to alleviate my pain, my guilt or my grief. And yet, through a twist of fate, that is exactly what he did. I'm sure he would never dream of the impact his simple *scrap* had on a total stranger.

A Returned Favour

Batoul Khanoom had worked for us for many years, 22 years, to be precise. She would come two to three times a week to cook, clean and occasionally do the weekly shopping for us. Everything she did came from the kindness of her heart and the generosity of her spirit. She wasn't just a cook and a cleaner, she nourished us with her love, her care and of course her beyond-delicious meals.

Normally, she never expected anything other than her wages and wasn't demanding in any way. The only time she ever asked for something was during the early years. She needed a winter coat and asked me if I could give her one. Her daughter's wedding was approaching and she needed something a bit more formal. I happily obliged, since I had one that had never been worn and had been sitting in the wardrobe for too long. I was glad that it was finally going to be useful, so I was delighted to give it to her.

Years passed. One day, Batoul Khanoom came to me and asked if I could give her what would be considered a relatively large amount of money. I can't remember exactly why she needed it. I vaguely recall that she wanted to go to a well-known private doctor, as her knee pain had become unbearable. She knew that there was a good chance she needed an operation and wanted it done by an experienced doctor. I felt for her, as I knew how hard it must have been for her to ask. All her children were very well-to-do but did absolutely nothing to help their mother. This saddened me deeply. At the time, the sum she requested was quite substantial for me and I knew this wasn't a loan. Her circumstances would never allow her to pay it back. I needed time to reflect before responding, given that the amount was equivalent to what I would typically earn in one month and I worked equally hard to make a living. My own personal circumstances had also changed. At the time, I was retired from a reputable university in Tehran after working there for over 35 years and was working for a private university. The pay, although it helped with the cost of living, wasn't as good as I used to receive before my voluntary retirement.

In the end, I knew that the right thing to do was to give her what she had asked for, so I did. She would never have asked me for something like that if it wasn't absolutely necessary. She was proud in the most positive sense of the word and I admired her character and work ethic.

A couple of months passed. One day at work, I heard a few colleagues talking about bonuses. The university had decided to make up for the lack of bonuses in the last few years, by soon giving generous bonuses to everyone. This came as a pleasant surprise so, I asked when this was due. 'Sorry, you're not entitled to it as you're retired from a different university,' said one of my colleagues. 'Never mind' I thought. 'It would have been nice but I'm not going to lose sleep over it.'

A week later, I received an email advising me to collect my bonus. I didn't take any notice of it. I thought it was a general email sent to everyone, not addressed to me personally, so I ignored it. A fortnight passed and this time, someone from HR came to me in person and asked me to go to the office and claim my bonus. I didn't question him but, still not convinced, I ignored this too. Then I received a phone call from the office and was told my bonus was ready and waiting for collection. By this third message I was totally confused. 'Wasn't I told that I wasn't entitled?'

Finally, I decided to go to the office to straighten things out. When I arrived, I was asked to give my name. As soon as I said it, I was informed that I was not entitled to this bonus because I was receiving retirement from another university. 'I knew that', I said and explained to the lady that I had only come to the office because of the constant messages and wanted to clear the issue once and for all. She wasn't sure either, so she asked me to wait while she checked her files.

Surprised, she said: 'Oh, they must have made a mistake. They have processed a bonus for you too.' I wasn't sure if I should accept it, since it was an error, but she insisted that it was best to take it now that it was issued or it would cause more confusion to send it back. In that case, I was happy to collect my cheque.

I left the office and glanced to see how much it actually was. When I saw it, I couldn't believe my eyes. This was the exact amount I had given Batoul Khanoom, with a little extra, almost as if it were interest!

I immediately thought, '***What goes around, comes around***'. I hold the strong belief that what we do or give to others comes back to us, whether it is good or bad! To witness it happen so soon and in such an unexpected way, was incredible. It was as if the universe was communicating with me directly, telling me to never withhold from a generous act, as there is always enough to go around.

Every time I remember this experience, I feel a warmth and a sense of security that I cannot describe. Years later, when I shared this story with a Canadian friend, she said: 'You're describing what we call *a wink from God*.' It struck me as a perfect way to describe such a synchronistic experience.

The Move

I was never prepared for what hit me after my divorce. I knew I wasn't happy and needed to find myself, but I had never anticipated the growing pains that would follow. My entire world collapsed when I left my husband after hanging on to my marriage for over 14 years. My new relationship was shaky and there was lots of emotional turbulence as I tried to make sense of the new person in my life, while grieving the end of my family unit. My daughter, who was ten at the time, did her best to adjust, but she too went through a massive inner earthquake. For two years after the divorce, I was lost in so many ways. I couldn't recognise myself. The image and all the ideas I had about myself kept crumbling down day after day. I thought I was strong, confident, able to take on the world and yet, I found myself on many occasions sobbing for hours, filled with confusion, self-hatred and insecurities I never knew I had. In those two stormy years, I rented out my flat and my daughter and I moved in with my new partner. Then, following a big argument, we moved out and I stayed with a friend while my daughter stayed with her father. This didn't stop the break-up, make up mode of my new romantic relationship. The way my life was panning out was not at all how I had envisaged it. What had I done? One thing was clear: I didn't want my old life back, but what I was living was no paradise either. I was at my wit's end!

Then one day, I woke up as if from a dream when an acquaintance whom I crossed paths with on the road casually brought up how crucial the teenage years were in the development of our children. As soon as I heard her say those words, I sensed deep in my gut, that I had to pull myself together for my daughter's sake or it would be too late. In all the emotional turmoil of that period, I had missed the fact that, with the increase in my salary, I could now rent a flat within walking distance of my daughter's school, my work and her father's new place. The very thought that she could be close to him while living with me was reassuring.

So I began my search for a place to rent. The second flat the estate agent showed me was in a little charming block, hidden from view. As soon as we went in, I sensed that this flat, with its warmth, spaciousness and brightness was going to symbolise a fresh start. My on/off boyfriend at the time, who is now my life partner of over 20 years, came with me when I signed the contract and collected the keys. He immediately showed interest in moving in with me. It seemed we were going to try to live together again despite our rocky relationship. I was happy with that arrangement because the flat was in my name and if there were another argument, my daughter and I would not have to move again.

Indeed, that flat, in the heart of High Barnet, offered a true space for my inner rebirth. It was a slow process and like any birth, not without its pain. So much was discovered within its walls and gradually, through a lot of inner work (yoga, meditation, self-enquiry), with the help of many teachers online (Byron Katie, Gangagi, Eckhart Tolle, Papaji, Maharishi Mahesh Yogi…), I was able to tap into a sense of peace when needed.

When our landlord, a Greek Cypriot gentleman decided to sell, we wondered if we would ever find a place that we liked as much, not only in terms of space, location and price, but also for the feeling of comforting security. Despite the possibility of never finding such a home, given our rent had hardly increased in seven years, I decided to keep a sense of safety and stability within my own being by not letting these kinds of thoughts settle into my mind. It was too easy for such negative thoughts to linger. This was especially true after viewing more expensive flats that were half the size of ours and had no character whatsoever. However, I was adamant not to entertain them. I made a pact with myself: to keep my thoughts and beliefs in line with the reality that I aspired to. In order to stay in the right state of mind, I had to mentally or even physically at times, move myself away from those who, unintentionally, projected a sense of panic by making comments that implied there was little chance of finding a similar place. Despite their unsettling words, I held on to the belief that there was just as much chance of finding an even better property within our means.

In my mind, the ideal place would be spacious with bright rooms, parking spaces, plenty of storage, maybe a garage, a balcony or patio (all of which we currently had) without too much of a financial stretch either. Maybe I was dreaming, but even after a month of fruitless searching, I wasn't ready to give up.

One evening, as my partner and I exchanged reassuring words, we had a bit of a giggle asking Sai Baba (his guru) if he could arrange for us to live in an area called Hadley Wood. Now, that would be an upgrade! We both laughed as we knew very well that this was in no way possible. Hadley Wood, filled with exquisite woods and nature, was the millionaires' corner of High Barnet with luxury flats offered for as little as £4000 (nearly three times our budget) and as much as £28000 per month.

A few days later, I received a phone call from our agency advising us that a flat had become available in Hadley Green. We were super excited as this was getting closer to Hadley Wood and as its name implies, it was surrounded by greenery. Unfortunately, nothing about this small flat was a fit. As much as I wanted to remain optimistic, that evening, I did feel a dread. What if it was time to back down? What if my eagerness to find the 'perfect home' was stopping us from settling down? Yet, I really couldn't see myself living in any of the places we had viewed so far. What if we couldn't find what we liked? What then? Trying to keep our spirits high, we joked with Baba again and said: 'Sai Baba, you misunderstood us, we didn't say Hadley Green, we said Hadley Wood' and repeated the words 'Hadley Wood' aloud a few times. We had a laugh and fell asleep with mixed emotions in our hearts.

The next day, I resumed my search online. My partner wanted me to be happy and trusted my choice, he was easygoing in this respect. On one level, that was wonderful because I knew if I was happy, he would be too. But at the same time, I felt the pressure, knowing it was my choosiness that was slowing the process. I kept an open mind as I looked at the details of each property, but by now, I knew the market inside out and none matched my specific requirements. That day, one flat kept coming up in all my different searches but, I really didn't like the metal staircase to the entrance next to a garage. Not only was I not tempted to look at the details of this property, I almost pushed it away mentally. Despite being aware of my particularity, I didn't want to be swayed towards something I really disliked. On my way back from work, I walked passed an estate agency and looked at the property photos in the window, in case anything jumped out. The agent who knew what I was looking for signalled me in. I went in and he showed me the one with the ugly entrance and said that it was in Camlet Way. I had no idea where that was and explained why I didn't like it but, he insisted that it was worth viewing.

Ever since our move into our current flat, I had taken the inner attitude of this is 'my home', 'my life' and it is up to me to keep order within it. I had created some strong boundaries which allowed me to feel safe and comfortable. Times had changed though, this wasn't the same situation as seven years ago. My daughter was older and my partner and I were much closer. I needed their support and valued their opinions, so there was no need to do this on my own. I decided to ask my daughter and partner what they thought about this property despite my initial resistance. So when I went home, I showed my daughter the property online to hear her thoughts. She was just waking up from an afternoon nap, she glanced at the photos with half-opened eyes and to my surprise said, 'Oh, that's cute!' Cute was the last word I would ever use to describe that property. However, seeing it through her eyes, I was tempted to consider viewing it. When my partner came home shortly after, I showed it to him too. I couldn't believe it when he said: 'Oh, that's Camlet Way, in

Hadley Wood. We must go and see it!' Was I hearing it right? Did I hear Hadley Wood? Was Sai Baba having a joke on us? Hadley Wood couldn't possibly have a flat within our means! Our excitement started bubbling up and we all decided to view it the next morning. So far letting my guard down and coming out of my protective shell had paid off. We were choosing our new home *together* as a united family. Clearly, this *unwanted* move had started healing past wounds.

When we arrived outside the flat, I realised that it was located on a road that, for years, as we drove along it, I would jokingly say 'I'd love to live here one day' and pick different houses I would happily live in! This one flat was part of an old mansion that was now divided into four properties. As soon as we entered and felt the space created by high ceilings and bright windows, we knew we loved it. We stood first in the modernised kitchen and as far as the eye could see, we saw trees and beautiful views from both large sash windows. Both bedrooms were spacious, one was en-suite and the other was larger than our then living room. There was so much character everywhere we looked! This was all that we had wished for and a lot more, plus with a bit of juggling, it wasn't too much of a stretch financially.
This became our home for the next seven years.

Life is showing me, more and more, that magic and miracles are part of all of our daily lives, whether we choose to see them or not. How is it that our little joke/prayer was answered this way? We never imagined it was possible. I wish I knew how prayer and intent work or, maybe I don't? Maybe I prefer the mystery and the element of surprise.

Every time I am reminded of how we found this flat one day after saying 'Hadley Wood' laughingly aloud a few times, I am filled with awe. Looking back at the experience, my eyes sparkle with light and my heart opens with trust, leaving me less frightened of the unknown.

This is definitely a great reminder that sometimes, when something is taken away, it is only to make room for something better. Remembering this, fully grasping this truth, may help us avoid deep suffering caused by changes and endings. There is no denying that endings can be hard; I've had many. But, I also know that without endings, there are no new and better beginnings, each with the potential to uncover more of ourselves.

And so, I'm learning to welcome change not as a threat, but as a doorway to something potentially greater.

Earrings

My mother came to see me in London in 2024 once she had her Canadian passport and was free to travel without the complications of applying for a UK visa. The last time I had seen her was before she left Iran for good in 2018. Obtaining her 'freedom passport' meant that borders were no longer as limiting and far more countries would now welcome her. Same person, different nationality, a totally different travel experience.

This meant that we could both go and visit her university friends in Paris while she was staying with us – friends whom she had made over 50 years ago within Sorbonne's historic walls. My heart melted seeing her reunite with her precious lifelong friends after 20 years. I had heard my mother on many occasions say that she didn't want to go to Paris and she felt no pull or need for it. She had been there, lived there for about 15 years and had gone back to visit to attend conferences a few times. She clearly stated that she was happy never to return. I believed her and I know this was her truth at the time – when obtaining a visa was practically impossible. But when she could, when the option was there, she didn't hesitate. Paris had planted the seed of the person she became. It had nourished her, helped her blossom and had gifted her friends with whom she shared a priceless bond.

Our visit to Paris was filled with love, laughter, tears of joy and even sadness as old memories were revisited and new ones shared. 20 years is indeed a lifetime! During those unforgettable four days, my mum's 'love cup', as she puts it, was fully replenished. It touched my heart to see how resilient they all were. Life has had its way with all of them and as Khalil Gibran would say, they had all been assigned to life's *'sacred fire'* in one way or the other and yet, they stood strong and loving, choosing gentleness over any bitterness. To say it was an enriching journey is an understatement.

When we came back, I wanted to send a little gift to my mum's Cypriot friend, who hosted us as a token of appreciation for her kindness and generosity. As my mum and I shopped around in London, I looked for earrings for Yolla, as I'd seen her wear a different pair every day. I finally found one she might like and bought it on 8th April, one day before my mother flew back to Canada. The earrings stayed on my shelf for a few days and realising I might get used to seeing them and forget to send them altogether, I put them in my purse as an attempt to remember. Each time I planned to go to the post office, something came up. Eventually, I saw very faint signs of the wrapping wearing off and I worried I would not be able to send them if it became any worse. Finally, on 18th April I made special efforts to send them.

A few days later, I received a beautiful 'thank you' message from Yolla, who also asked me to call her at my convenience. When I called her, she told me that she had something to share, which could be suitable for the book she knew I was writing – a seeming coincidence that had brought her much joy:
On her birthday, the 22nd April, she had received an unexpected gift by post. The earrings I had sent her, without knowing the date, had arrived on the very day! I couldn't believe it.

Many times I have arranged for a gift or a card to arrive on a special occasion, only to find out that it arrived a day or two out of sync despite my genuine efforts. This time the timing was perfect, even though I had no idea it was her birthday. My delays and lack of organisation, as if orchestrated from above, had her receive her present exactly on her special day.

This fills me with gratitude and trust that everything happens at exactly the right time, for exactly the right reasons.

Perfumed with Grace

For me, wearing perfume is an essential part of feeling fresh and lively. I spray it every time I apply my make-up, ready to embrace the world with a joyful heart. A pleasant fragrance can transport me to a different place for a while, giving a profound sense of well-being. I wear perfume for myself, for the spring it puts in my step.

For many years, my financial circumstances allowed me to buy any perfume that I desired. Buying perfume used to be as effortless as grabbing a bottle of water, a luxury I never had to think twice about. As fate would have it, my buying power changed drastically and buying my favourite perfume was no longer within my means. I still had some left in the bottle but every time I wore it, I felt a tinge of sadness, knowing I wouldn't be able to replace it. There were far more important things to replace and a bottle of perfume was the least of my priorities.

Later on, while still unable to afford perfume, I became drawn to the scent of Oud and loved smelling it on others. Somehow, it took me back to the past and for reasons that escape me, it gave me a sense of warmth and safety. I told myself that when the page turned and my buying power returned, I would choose one with Oud as its main fragrance.
Even just imagining it brought me joy.

One day, a friend came to visit, bringing me a present. When I unwrapped it and opened the box, I was absolutely stunned. It was my favourite brand, but with the scent of Oud. Seeing my shocked face, another friend who had helped choose the gift said: 'Oh, isn't this your favourite perfume?' She knew I wore that brand but wasn't sure which one. I said: 'No, no, it is the brand that I wear, but not this scent.' They reassured me it could be exchanged, thinking they'd made a mistake. I chuckled. I told them they had no idea how happy they'd made me because it was the very perfume I'd been dreaming of and I hadn't even known it existed: My perfume brand with my new favourite scent! Had it not been for their *mistake*, my wish wouldn't have come true.

I don't know how this happened, but this meant the world to me. It wasn't just about the perfume; it was much more than that. This happened at a time when I had no choice but to adapt to unexpected life changes that evoked feelings of grief, shock and disappointment. Yet, the bottle I held in my hand was a testament that my needs and desires could be met, even in the midst of a financial crisis. It gave me the stamina I needed to face the ongoing difficulties with renewed hope and trust.

Ten

In October 2017, I listened to 'The Power of Meaning' by Emily Esfahani Smith after friends who knew the author's family recommended it. Listening to it on Audible while walking around our neighbourhood in Hadley Wood, Hertfordshire, evoked a sense of wholeness. In her book she argues that finding meaning can add an immeasurable depth to our lives, which is far more fulfilling than the pursuit of personal happiness. The search for meaning, in her views, is not some esoteric pursuit requiring you to travel to a distant monastery to figure out life's great secret. We can tap into unexplored sources of meaning all around us – right here, right now. Drawing on the latest research in positive psychology, on insights from George Eliot, Viktor Frankl, Aristotle, the Buddha and other great minds; and on interviews with seekers of meaning, Emily lays out the four pillars that give meaning to our lives: belonging, purpose, storytelling and transcendence.

The inspiring words of Emily, combined with the breathtaking autumnal scenery, brought about optimistic vibes, as I strolled up and down the hilly roads. As I walked, I spotted a house near our flat that had been for sale for at least a year. For some unknown reason, I decided to explore around the house. As my curiosity grew, I peeked through the windows and checked out its empty rooms. Looking back, I am not sure what it was about the house that was calling me. Maybe it was the silence that surrounded it as it had been empty for a while or, maybe it was the memories within its walls.

At the time, I had no idea that what I was about to do was trespassing and against the law. It was only when I recounted the story to my other half that I realised it was a true faux-pas, and I could have easily been arrested. Oops!

I looked through the metal gate into the garden. Not far from the gate, stood two beautiful trees with rare cherry-like fruits that I had never seen before. I was intrigued; I opened the gate and entered what felt like an enchanted space. There I was, feeling like Alice in Wonderland, open to adventures. I walked down with gentle steps to the end of the garden, not wanting to disturb its calm. Leaning against a tall tree, I absorbed the tranquil energy around me. On my right-hand side, the garden merged with a magnificent field covered by a blanket of wildflowers. On my left stood this beautiful Tudor style house that would be at least a 100 years old. All my senses had come to life. The breeze felt like a messenger of peace, brushing my skin, as I stood immersed in deep contemplation.

Up to that point, I had always lived in flats with balconies or patios that I could decorate with lots of pots of flowers. Having a garden was never a priority. It is so true what they say: 'You can't miss what you never had'. As I leaned on that tree though, I began pondering the possibility of having such a garden. I could see in my mind's eye children and adults playing on the grass filled with the joy of being alive and connected. The idea of my own garden becoming a hub for playfulness and connection, as well as a little haven of nature, made my heart sing. The desire for a garden was ignited in a way I had never felt before.

Then, the serene house caught my attention; she was a beauty, yet showed very clear signs of being tired and neglected. As crazy as it sounds, I began to have what felt like a genuine and called-for conversation with the house. It seemed to me that every word I uttered in my heart was being heard by this presence. Completely conscious of the fact that this house was way above my pay grade, I said to her: 'If you want me to tend and care for you, give me the means that would allow me to do so; I will take good care of you.' I knew I was heard, her presence was undeniably alive. As odd as it may sound, the house and I shared an intimate moment and, without a doubt, there was a quiet depth in our exchange.

Walking back towards the gate, I sensed a certain magic in the air.

I left the garden with a poise that had a quality I had never felt before. It must have been the calm of a secure and prosperous heart, awake to the potential of all needs being met. Once back in the street, I felt like a little girl who had just opened a very precious gift in the form of a special message:

'***Anything is possible!***'

Weeks passed and I shared my experience with my other half and a few friends. It was as if I was preparing them, in case, by some miracle, the house would choose us as its next occupants. A part of me knew how ludicrous the thought was as the house was over £3,000,000 and at a stretch, our current finances would allow for a house worth £600,000. The other part, though, enjoyed playing lightheartedly with the magic I had sensed in that garden.

One night, just as I was falling asleep, I felt the spirit of the house and had an epiphany; or perhaps not an epiphany, more like a message: 'All of the numbers of places you have lived in the UK, for the past 25 years added up to or were ten. You have lived in flat number 10, 46, 73, 37 and you are now living in number 82.'
How could I have missed this before?
There was more to this intriguing message: 'Tomorrow, go and check the number of the house you have your eyes on. If it adds up to 10, the house can be yours; if not, let it go.' I was amused and giggled to myself, like a child playing with an invisible friend - at 50! With a playful smile and a trusting heart, I fell asleep.

Needless to say, my first move the next morning was to walk to the house before work. I approached it hesitantly as there was a chance, a big chance that the number could be 73. It didn't take long to see that it wasn't after all and unfortunately 75 didn't add up to ten. I cannot say that I was disappointed, quite the opposite. I felt the message had started a game that was leading somewhere interesting. If this house wasn't to be mine because its numbers didn't add up to ten, did that mean that the number of the house I was meant to have would? I was curious, I knew that I wasn't given this information for no reason. Deep down, I was sure, it meant something.

As fate would have it, the house was sold by the end of the same week after being on the market for over a year. I was grateful that I had already let go of it and my daydream wasn't abruptly interrupted by seeing the new occupants move in. I thanked my messenger for showing me before that the game with the house was over and in my heart, wished the new occupants good luck. My desire for a magical house with a garden stayed and I felt that some invisible force was at work to make it happen.

A few months later, our landlord told us that he was selling the flat we had rented. If we were meant to have a house with a garden, this was our chance. This was the time to start taking all the necessary actions to make that dream a reality.

We viewed about 15 properties and each time, I was drawn to check their numbers to see if they added up to ten. We had many criteria for our new place and we weren't going to let the number of the house reduce our chances of finding a suitable home. To base our decision on a message that I had received would have been too illogical and childlike but, it didn't stop me checking.

After months of looking, we finally placed an offer on a glorious ground floor flat with high ceilings in a gorgeous setting. The terrace windows of the living room opened to a listed historic park which served as the communal garden. We couldn't care less that the flat number was two; we loved the feel of the place and the open view from the living room. A part of me wondered why I had been given that message but I couldn't take that too seriously and anyway, I convinced myself that during my childhood, we had lived twice in a number two.

We were utterly disappointed when our offer was rejected, as we didn't think we could increase it. We carried on our search but soon realised that our budget was too low for what we were looking for. A conversation with our mortgage broker made us see that it was possible to increase it.

The last property we saw in 2019 was a house with a charming garden. It was a dream house, it ticked all the boxes, every single one and we bought it in 2020. To add a bit of magic to our purchase, the number of this house does add up to ten.
We now live in number 19.

I don't know what it was that showed me, in the darkness of an evening before sleep, what my previous addresses and my future house had in common. Whatever it was, in its mysterious playfulness, it opened my eyes to something in the past I had never noticed before and to something in the future that was waiting for me.

Unveiling the Verse

It was 19 March 2023 and I was setting up a special table in preparation for the Persian New Year (Norooz), which was happening the following day. Norooz, also celebrated in countries like Turkey and Afghanistan, is based on the Persian calendar and marks the spring equinox. On this table, we arrange small dishes filled with symbolic foods that represent life, health, love and prosperity.

Traditionally, many families include the 'Divan e Hafiz,' a collection of poems by Hafiz, who holds a spiritual authority for many. His words are read either before or after the countdown to the new year. Traditionally, his book is used for a reading, much like drawing a card from an oracle deck, to seek general guidance or advice on current matters. There is a whole ritual around it: we hold – or better say, we almost hug – the book, say a special prayer as we invite Hafiz's spirit, kiss the closed pages as we run our fingers gently over the top until we are guided to open a certain page. In the reading we always find pearls of wisdom whether we feel it is completely relevant to our specific question or not.

I have a few of his collections, given to me as a gift, some with commentaries, some without. Some with special calligraphy and illustrations, some without. I was deciding which to put on the table for this celebration when an illustrated book drew my attention. The colours seemed to match the theme perfectly, so I decided to use that one.

The cover of the book was an image with half of a line from one of his poems, but the calligraphy which wasn't written in a straight line made it challenging to read. With a bit of effort, I managed to decipher all the words but wasn't sure of the order or clear on the meaning. I really wanted to understand what it said but, knowing how much I had to do, I decided not to spend too long on it and put the book down. A few minutes later, I realised I couldn't let it go as my curiosity grew stronger about the meaning of this half-line. I had to know the rest of the poem. So instead of resisting my obsession, I went with it and began looking for it.

It's usually easy to find a specific poem in his 500-poem collection, as they are alphabetically sorted by the last letters and each line of a poem ends with the same letters throughout. Provided you know the last half of a line, you can find the poem in no time. I spent a while searching but my task proved more difficult than I anticipated. One, I wasn't sure of the order of my words, two, I didn't know if what I had was the first or second half of a line. Despite many attempts to rearrange the order of the words, I had no luck finding this mysterious poem that had hooked me.

I had a lot on my to-do list and as it was, I had already spent enough time being distracted by the pull of this poem. I knew I had to stop indulging my curiosity and carry on with the serious task of getting ready for the next day. Determined, I put the book back on the table and continued with my preparations. A few minutes later, out of the blue, a different word order popped into my head, one I had not considered before. It was worth a shot. I couldn't help but pick the book up again, hoping I had found the key.

This time, it took seconds to find it. It was the 18th poem (ghazal) of his book. As it turned out, the half-line responsible for my fixation, was halfway through the poem. So, I made myself comfortable and with great anticipation, started reading. I wondered if there was an important message for me hidden in its lines. The first line I read made me gasp in surprise – I couldn't believe the relevance! It read:

Oh, Saghi, may the dawn of the new year bring blessings to you,
May the vows you've made remain carved in your heart, ever true.

Out of 500 poems, there was a 0.2% chance of finding one that began with a blessing for the new year. It wasn't just that, I was nudged and nudged again to find and read this poem. It felt deeply personal. Time stood still and tears of gratitude welled up. As I read the entire poem, I sensed I was in the presence of a great being who cared for and guided me.

I took this seriously and called a friend who knows Persian literature and Hafiz better than I do. Reading Hafiz is a bit like reading Shakespeare; unless you are familiar with his work and have some background knowledge, you won't fully understand it. So, I asked my friend to explain each line – in plain language. The poem which was very heart-warming came with a message. The main message - apart from the blessings of the new year – was advice to hold on to my Noah's Ark. As long as I held onto my inner resources and what I believed in, all would be well. Otherwise, the coming events could sweep the ground from under my feet and uproot me. I thanked my friend and took the advice on board.

And yes, what came a few days later was big, huge in fact, with many challenging and heart-wrenching emotions. I found out that someone very close and special to me had lost his home in the most humiliating way which involved bailiffs. He had to borrow money from a friend to rent a place urgently or he'd end up on the street. He is vulnerable and his financial decisions are made by others which had in this case, backfired big time.

With Hafiz's words in mind and his timely poem echoing within me, I stayed vigilant and true to everything that anchored me. His message gave me the boost of confidence I needed and reminded me that my inner Noah's Ark was powerful enough to save me from drowning under the turbulent waves of unfolding events.

Where do these messages that carry a unique quality, come from? They are often received with a sense of urgency or mystery recognised only by the intended receiver. Where do they come from?

I must live and enjoy the many questions for which I have no answer. Still I do know this: once a personal message is truly received, it sets the inner compass and leads to a gentler journey.

Redundancy

We went camping on the Isle of Wight, a holiday we had booked before I was made redundant. It marked a significant period in my life, as I contemplated leaving my career in IT (Information Technology). It wasn't an easy decision, considering my hard-earned degree and over four years working with an International Software company. Despite being promoted twice, I was ultimately let go after the fourth round of redundancies. During our holiday, I spent a lot of time reflecting on the kind of life and work I truly wanted.

Two years prior to that, I'd realised I was playing a role in fulfilling someone else's dream. I had a strong sense that I didn't belong in the corporate world and if I stayed, a deep part of me wasn't going to flourish in that industry. Naturally, I had reservations about leaving a career with a well-paved path and I knew I had a lot of soul-searching to do to find out my next steps.

In spite of that, underneath the doubts and fears that lingered in my mind, there was a deep sense of peace. Perhaps because we were away, surrounded by natural beauty and serenity. I wasn't going to spend all my time thinking of the future, instead, I embraced every moment and enjoyed one of my best holidays. What had happened was out of my control but it was the catalyst I needed to make the changes I had wanted for a while. I had surrendered and was open to the next chapter of my life.

As ready as I felt, a synchronicity confirmed my sense of self-assurance which left no room for doubt that the universe had my back! This is what happened:

We never ate out when we went camping. Our ritual was to have a barbecue every night by the tent. We'd go to the nearest supermarket to buy all the necessary ingredients, including drinks, in preparation for our dinner. Typically, my husband at the time would get beers and

I would pick up some wine. However, that day, I decided not to buy any wine, thinking I didn't need to drink every night.

As evening fell, we made our barbecue under the stars and sat inside the tent, enjoying our delicious meal. My daughter had found new friends and was having a fabulous time eating and laughing with them. Enjoying the heart-warming scene, I glanced at her father contentedly sipping his cool beer and suddenly regretted not buying my white wine. I said: 'Shame! I should have gotten the wine, I really fancy some now.' Within minutes, we heard a voice behind our zipped tent door. 'Hello' the voice said. We unzipped the door and there he was: Our camping neighbour holding a half-empty bottle of white wine. Up until then, apart from the polite hellos, we hadn't really spoken. He said: 'We're leaving early morning tomorrow and it's best if we don't drink tonight. It would be a shame to waste what's left in the bottle. Would you like it?' I had a massive smile on my face and shared how I had just expressed my regret for not buying any wine in the afternoon. I was thrilled! I thanked him and gladly accepted the bottle.

I poured a glass and as I was about to take my first sip, I felt immense gratitude for life. My fulfilled wish for a glass of white wine may have been very small compared to losing my job but, it certainly put everything into perspective. It gave me a deep conviction that everything was as it should be and would ultimately work out in my favour.

It was loud and clear: the universe did have my back!

The Enigmatic Shift

Years ago, I went to New York City and reached out to an old friend, hoping to catch up with him. It had been 30 years since he'd moved to America and since we had last met in England. Our communication had been sporadic and apart from an odd email once in a blue moon, we hadn't been in touch.

I contacted him and was delighted that he was eager to meet. He suggested getting together the same evening despite having just returned from his honeymoon that afternoon. I wanted to give him more time to settle back in, but he was adamant about meeting and introducing me to his new wife sooner rather than later. So, we met that evening and had the most extraordinary conversation.

As we sat down to catch up, I noticed a significant change in his demeanour. Back in England, when he was around 20 years old, he had been known among my brothers and our group of friends for his wild and extravagant lifestyle, indulging in champagne, fancy cars and all the luxuries money could buy. He was always treating everyone to drinks, being he was the only one who could afford to. As a stockbroker in the city, he was earning obscene amounts while we were all earning next to nothing. However, his drinking habits and the resulting behaviours drove many of his friends away. Despite all this, I held onto the belief that he had goodness underneath his chaotic behaviour.

During our conversation, he opened up and told me about his transformation since moving to America. He had joined Alcoholics Anonymous (AA) and had successfully broken free from his alcohol addiction. This wasn't all – he also told me that he had found God. I nearly fell off my chair as I couldn't believe these words were coming out of his mouth. He was, after all, one of the wildest, most reckless men you could possibly imagine! I was captivated.

He went on to describe the pivotal moment that changed the course of his life forever. He had been offered a lucrative job by a prestigious American bank, Cazenovia. Normally, he would have jumped at such a golden opportunity, because back then, it was all about money, money and more money. His personal motto at the time was, 'The more you earn, the better it gets.' As he recounted the story, his tone became more contemplative, as if he were reliving the past. He explained how, contrary to his usual inclinations and much to his own surprise, he declined this once-in-a-lifetime offer and chose to stick to his current job, even though it meant earning considerably less money. He couldn't understand why, despite the fact that this was the ideal job in every sense, with fortunes to be earned, he felt compelled to turn it down. In his own words: '*Something* was making me say no.'

Just two days after his decision, the tragic events of 9/11 occurred and the Cazenovia offices, located in the World Trade Centre, were destroyed. He believed that a higher power had intervened, sparing him from a catastrophic end. This was when he felt a profound connection with God, which essentially led him to turn his life around, leave behind his reckless past and fully embrace sobriety and spirituality.

Listening to David's incredible journey, I couldn't help but feel awe and respect for the man he had become. His transformation was nothing short of miraculous, proving that even the wildest of souls could find peace and start afresh. I had always liked David; he was fun to be around, but from that evening, I cherished our friendship even more.

He gave me hope that it's never too late to turn the ship around no matter how far off course it's gone.

The Lost Keys

I arrived bright and early, eager for the second part of my Thai Massage course. None of the other six participants who had completed the first part with me had arrived yet. The course was taking place at my teacher's house, where I had been many times before to receive massages from his daughter.

That day, he wasn't his usual self. Stressed and frustrated, he explained that he had spent the last three days looking for his car keys with no luck. He had spent hours searching everywhere, but couldn't understand how they had mysteriously vanished into thin air. Much to my own surprise, I told him with *great confidence* that I would find the keys for him at the end of the day, when we finished our session. He liked the sound of that but repeated that there was nowhere in the house he hadn't looked. In my heart of heart, I was sure I would find them, but I had no idea where my conviction came from. It was such a strong, unshakable knowing that didn't leave any room for doubt.

When the day of learning and practicing ended, one of the other students asked me if I could give him a lift. I apologised and said I couldn't, as I had promised to look for the lost keys. Our teacher, who had shared his frustration with the class a couple of times during the day, overheard me. He made me accountable in front of everyone, telling them that I was convinced I'd find them. His tone was certainly hopeful but also had a tint of sarcasm – a tone that seemed to say: 'You must be dreaming, but if you do find it, I'll be over the moon.'

What had I got myself into? Why had I made such a bold claim? This wasn't the time for doubt, so when the others left, we went through the motions. I asked the usual questions: 'when did you have them last? What did you do after?' etc. After coming home from a fair to promote his work, he had carried lots of bags from the car to a storage room. I looked in every corner of that room. We went back and forth to the car. We checked in and around the house. While he answered my questions as we moved through the rooms, I couldn't help but notice his reluctance. Not because he didn't want me in the rooms – he's not the private type – but because he was annoyed that we were repeating the same steps he had already taken a 100 times on his own. A deep part of me wanted to help and to stay loyal to my intuitive conviction and yet, I didn't really know *how* or *if* I could keep my promise. I didn't want to force anything as I didn't have anything to prove. The words that had come out of my mouth that morning, hadn't come from my ego. They were just spoken out of a deep knowing.

After about five minutes, I decided not to insist and risk causing more frustration for the poor man. Maybe I was wrong, so I decided to leave him in peace. I grabbed my trainers and for the first time ever, sat on the stairs to put them on. I had not once done that in all the times that I had visited their house. From where I sat, my eyes levelled with the floor under the low table by the front door. There, right at the back, next to the wall, I saw something. I got up, reached for it and handed him the keys. We were both flabbergasted! He was overjoyed to finally find his keys and be able to drive after three days of being stuck at home. I was ecstatic to see that my inner knowing was something I could indeed trust.

He was full of praise that evening, the next day and the next… As much as he wanted to give me the credit and as much as a part of me enjoyed it, I knew that I couldn't make this success about me. Finding the keys wasn't *my* doing. Something beyond me had made me sit down on those stairs instead of standing to put my trainers on as I usually do. Had I not done that, I wouldn't have seen them.

I offer my gratitude and deepest respect to whatever it was that prompted me to help and end his frustration.

Riddle of Goodbye

It was October 2004 when my grandmother, Mahin, was hospitalised after a series of falls caused by several mini-strokes. She had also developed dementia, which was progressively getting worse. My brother, mother and I took turns visiting her every day. Though she didn't always recognise us, we knew who she was and how important she had been in shaping us all.

On her birthday, while she was in the hospital, we took a small cake and a few presents to celebrate the special day with her. Her birthday, which fell on the 4th of Aban in the Persian Calendar (25th Oct), coincided with the birthday of the last king in Iran – something she always took pride in.

She was delighted to see us all but she seemed unsure about the occasion. I wished her a happy birthday and asked if she knew the date. She replied that it wasn't her birthday and insisted her birthday was on the 17th of Aban (7th Nov). She repeated this several times holding her ground so we went along with it to avoid causing her unnecessary distress.

Sadly, this turned out to be the last time I heard her speak. She developed severe pneumonia, which unexpectedly worsened and she passed away a few days later. Astonishingly, she passed on the day she had insisted was her birthday: The 17th of Aban (7th Nov). We were awestruck!

Did she have a premonition of some sort? Was it just a coincidence that she confused the day she was born with the day she would die? Did that mean that her death was a birth in another realm? Why would she even mention it? We were left with so many questions but no answer.

While we were grieving, the fact that she had spoken of the date of her death gave the experience a surreal, almost mystical quality. It felt as though, in her final days, she had access to a knowing we couldn't comprehend. The mystery of her passing on the exact date she was convinced was her birthday had a profound impact on all of us. It didn't stop the pain of losing her but it certainly prompted us to question what we believe about life and death and to delve beyond our usual understanding.

The Gift of Connection

Our cat Milly was a birthday gift for my daughter on her 9th birthday. I still remember the first time I saw her. My then husband brought her home, opened the box and a little golden ginger cat jumped out. Before Milly, I didn't particularly like ginger cats, but after watching her sniff around and explore her new territory with a curiosity that only cats possess, I fell in love with her.

Milly was an amazing cat in so many ways. She shared many pivotal moments with our family, including my divorce and five different moves. She adapted to each new place without fuss and was generally an easygoing companion – truly kind, beautiful and no trouble at all. She rarely needed visits to the vet.

At the time, I thought it would be kind to let her have a litter before being spayed. When she was four, she gave birth to four beautiful boys, just two weeks before we moved into a new flat in a block at 37 Manor Road, Barnet. We made such wonderful memories with all five cats living with us, but deep down, we knew we couldn't keep them all. The tough decision was made to find new homes for the little ones once they turned eight weeks old. When the time came, we managed to re-home them over the course of two to three days. The first night without them was heartbreaking. I could feel Milly's pain as she called for her babies. I felt awful – cruel and guilty – for having separated them. I sensed her despair. I lay next to her, stroking her gently and quietly crying until she finally settled down.

Fast forward 15 years. We had been living in our new house for a year when we started noticing Milly's health was declining. She was, after all, an old lady cat. Though still beautiful, she showed clear signs that her time was approaching. Quietly, she withdrew from the world, struggling to eat and finding it hard to even walk to quench her thirst. With hope in our hearts, we took her to the vet, praying for a solution. They tentatively suggested that the kindest option would be to put her down, as she was suffering. As much as we wanted to hold on and delay saying goodbye, we knew it was the most compassionate choice. I held her closely, gently whispering loving words to her as she died in my arms.

She died two days before my birthday. In an attempt to console myself I tried to see if her passing had any hidden gift – a spiritual message – meant for me. I kept hearing – or perhaps imagining – her asking me 'to connect to Spirit'. 'I do', I thought. 'How can I connect more than I already do?' I caught myself constantly looking at the spot where she used to sleep when she was sick, feeling a deep void and overwhelming grief. Maybe by 'Connect to Spirit', she meant 'See me even as your physical eyes can't', so I began to entertain the idea. Every time I looked at the empty spot where she used to lie, I would imagine that it was filled with her invisible energy and spirit. This thought eased my pain, even if it may have been wishful thinking.

We knew we'd eventually get another cat when the time felt right. A couple of months after Milly had passed, a friend – who used to be our neighbour in Manor Road – mentioned that the person now living in our old flat was fostering kittens. She wanted to know if we were keen to see them. I asked if they were tabbies since I'd recently fallen in love with one and was adamant to have one this time. She said they were black and white, so I decided not to pursue it further. Besides, it turned out, that it wouldn't have been easy for us to go and see them even if we had chosen to do so.

Another friend, who is very much in touch with the 'other side', found out that we were thinking of getting a kitten sooner rather than later. She suggested that we ask Milly's permission before bringing another cat into the house. During our conversation, she said: 'I can see two kittens and not just one. It's probably nothing, maybe I'm just imagining it, but that's what I see.'

Asking for her permission? It's not the kind of thing I normally do but I thought it wouldn't hurt to ask in case she was indeed present on the other side. So, I said aloud: 'Milly, if you are happy for us to have a cat, please guide us to it and give us a sign that it is coming from you.'

A couple of months later, my husband suggested it was time to start actively looking. I began my search online for a rescue kitten and landed on a platform of charities featuring their tabbies. I chose two charities, one in Enfield and another near us in Hertfordshire. I called them both, completed online forms and waited for a response. One charity never replied, but the one in Enfield got back to me and scheduled a video call, instead of a home visit, due to lockdown restrictions. During the call, as soon as she heard we'd had cats before and how much we loved our Milly who was now buried in our garden, she sounded reassured.

Towards the end of the conversation, she cheerfully said: 'Great! I'll contact the foster home and will find out when you can see the kittens.' The charity was in Enfield so I had expected to go to Enfield to see them but as she had not mentioned where they were, I asked.

To my surprise, she replied: 'Barnet.'
'You don't – by any chance – mean Manor Road, do you?' I asked.
'Yeah!'
'It's not Number 37, is it?'
'Yes it is, how did you know?!'
In joyful disbelief I explained that I had heard the person living in our old home was fostering cats.

Out of all the possible charities on this platform - just one of hundreds online, with so many foster homes, I had unknowingly chosen our old flat where we lived for seven years. It was surreal to go back there after 14 years and pick the kittens from our old bedroom! As fate would have it, my friend's premonition was right: We brought home not just one but two kittens. It turned out that they were only offered in pairs as they were too young and bringing just one wasn't an option.

I had asked Milly to guide us to our next cat and show us that it was coming from her. It was as clear as the blue sky to me this was her blessing. The entire process felt orchestrated from beyond, guiding us back to our old home, where Milly had lovingly raised her four kittens, to bring two adorable cuties into our lives.

Thank you, Milly!
While Mishka and Leela could never replace you, we are very happy with your choice!
Thank you for showing us the way and for the gift of 'connection to spirit'.
We are forever grateful.

One Silk Pillowcase

There were other strange and mysterious events surrounding Milly and her passing, beyond the one mentioned in the previous story (The Gift of Connection). This one happened just after she passed.

It was pouring with rain and the dark clouds seemed to mirror the heaviness in our hearts. Even the weather matched our mood: Milly had just died peacefully in my arms at the vet.

We brought her home with us to bury her in our garden. I put her on the floor next to the garden door and went upstairs to fetch something to wrap her in. I thought of my silk pillow case as I wanted Milly to be wrapped in softness and love. I had cherished that pillowcase, a gift from a dear friend so, it felt right to give Milly something special rather than what I no longer needed. It took us hours to dig a deep hole. Finally, exhausted and heart-broken, we buried her and said our final goodbye.

My husband was as devastated as me and was also sad to see me give up my favourite pillowcase. He suggested that I buy another one but I didn't care. All that mattered at the time was that Milly had mine and that was enough.

The very next day as I checked my emails, I saw that I had received one from Evie@thisissilk.com. The subject read:
'One Silk Pillow Case.'

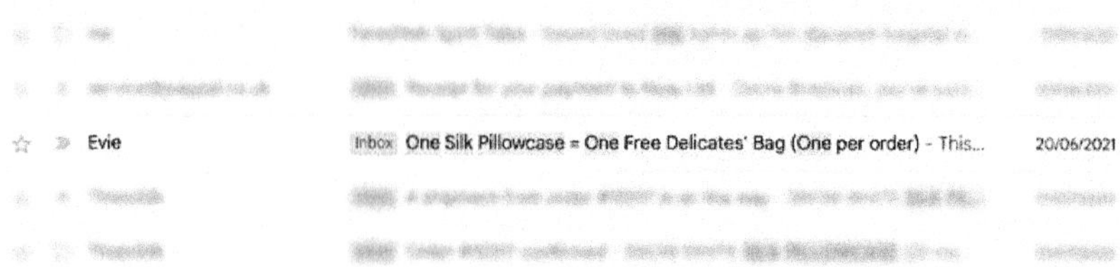

Up until then, I had never received any emails from This Is Silk where I bought a pillowcase for my daughter in 2020. They had my details but this was the very first time I received a promotional email from them. One day after I gave mine to Milly.
The timing was uncanny.

Tears welled up when I read the e-mail. It was an invitation to buy a silk pillow case. I could sense Milly's presence ever so strongly. It was as though *she* was the one asking me to replace it, to be kind to myself as I was to her and not do without what I liked. Even though I had never intended to buy one, I placed my order.

All the company wanted to do was to increase their sales through a newsletter, and they did. Could they imagine that their promotion could bring an intense sense of connection to something mysterious and beautiful? I doubt it.

It seems that mystery is always interwoven with the mundane. It is everywhere and acts and communicates in very personal ways, without anyone else noticing except the one for whom the message is intended – a silent testament to the unseen bonds that hold us together beyond space and time.

A Mother's Love

My mother passed away on 7 September 2006. We shared an incredibly close bond, a truly special connection. Needless to say, her death created a big void in my life and left me feeling lost and disoriented.

Around four to five weeks after her funeral, while I was deeply grieving her loss, reliving memories and struggling to sleep, something out of the ordinary began to happen. I started hearing her voice, which became clearer and more persistent, especially during the night. She would call my name with tender expressions over and over again. Was I going mad? Was it the grief and exhaustion playing tricks on me? It wasn't just her voice that I could so clearly hear, I could actually feel her physical presence. I truly thought I was on the brink of losing my sanity, so I reached out to some friends and family. They assured me that my experience was not unusual and that I was simply going through an intense sense of loss. I had to weather it till it passed.

Two or three months later, what I assumed was a hallucination hadn't stopped which was unsettling to say the least. On a Friday night, as I sat watching television, I heard her voice vividly as if she were sitting right next to me. Exhausted after a long and challenging week I decided to ignore it. I closed my eyes and took a short nap. Suddenly, I felt a breeze as if someone had just passed by. Her voice grew louder as she called my name.

I couldn't take it anymore so started pleading to her. Speaking aloud, I begged her to help me know that I wasn't losing my mind, by giving me a sign that it was indeed her and not my imagination running wild.
Back then, I had one of those first laptops that were clumsier than the ones we use now in 2023. It wasn't as fancy as the new laptops with a mouse pad that would respond at the gentlest touch. This one had a

red button in the middle of the keyboard instead, which had to be pressed hard enough to make any changes. My laptop, sitting on the coffee table nearby, had gone into hibernation mode. Usually, to reactivate it, I would have to press the red button hard, hear a click which would turn on both the screen and the fan.
In the midst of my plea, as I was begging my mother for a sign, tears streaming down my face, something happened that stopped the stream of my thoughts and settled my internal chaos.

I heard a click from my laptop, the screen lit up and the fan began to hum!

I was taken aback and yet felt a profound sense of peace. I wasn't mad after all! My experience was real, it was indeed her presence I was feeling and the clear sign I had so badly needed, was given. Something had pressed the red button for it to click, it required pressure! I was so calmed by this, that I didn't need to share it with anyone. She had convinced me and that was enough.

Until I went to work on Monday. The experience over the weekend had taken a load off my shoulders, to the point that even my staff noticed the shift in my demeanour. They were intrigued by how much lighter I was compared to the previous weeks. I glanced, smiling at a photo of my mother on the bookshelf and decided to tell the ladies what had brought about the change. They were already in the loop and knew how unsettling I had found hearing my late mother's voice. I briefly went through what happened on Friday. As I was recounting the story, one of the ladies, typically serious and dry, objected to the validity of my story, implying I was making it up or reading too much into it.

Just after she exclaimed 'Oh my God, I've heard it all now', we were jolted by a very loud bang on the bookshelf. It was a jarring noise, especially since we were the only ones in the office and no-one else was in the building. Struggling to understand what had just happened, we all looked at each other in utter surprise.

As I looked around I saw that the heavy frame which was on the bookshelf – with my mother's photo in it – had disappeared. I ran towards it and saw that it had fallen in a way that defied logic. It had landed in the most peculiar way, as though someone had deliberately lifted and placed it face down in its new position. No amount of pressure or shaking from behind the bookshelf could have made this happen. I am an engineer with strong spatial awareness so I knew how bizarre this fall looked and yet decided not to say anything. The skeptical lady was overwhelmed; she had also realised that there was something uncanny about this fall. She tried to figure out how this could have happened by testing different scenarios but couldn't come up with a rational explanation. She was so shaken that she excused herself and asked to leave the office, admitting that she needed time to process what had just happened. I suggested to the other lady to take the day off as well, as the atmosphere was no longer conducive to productivity.

In the days that followed, I tried different experiments myself, dropping the frame from its original place with impacts from different angles, but could never recreate the way that it had landed, nor the sound it had made.

I have no explanation for this, but I do know that when I was sharing my story, I was scoffed at and immediately after, my mother's frame fell and made a huge impact. I can't ignore the possibility that she was reasserting her presence and validating the authenticity of my story. Whether it was coincidence or something more, in my heart, I knew she was with me.

Let it Come to You

After weeks of clearing out and packing, we had finally moved into our new home, ready to unpack and settle down. The number of bags and boxes that went in and out of my car's boot, despite having professional movers, seemed countless. One evening, I brought a few big bags from my car, emptied and sorted their contents and then took the empty bags to the garage. When I realised that I had misplaced my car key, I assumed it must have fallen into one of the bags while I was carrying them inside. So, off I went to the garage, confident that I'd find it there. I searched everywhere, turned the bags inside out, shook them, inspected every corner, but it was nowhere to be found. I lost hope and decided to let it go, hoping that I would be able to find it the next day.

When I sat down to meditate the following morning, I felt tension rising as the thought of my lost key popped into my head. I returned my focus to my mantra and felt myself begin to relax. Then another thought arose: 'Maharishi Mahesh Yogi, my meditation teacher, always taught: 'Let things come to you. Don't tense up to achieve, relax and receive." As I remembered his message, I let go of worry, knowing that the key will come to me at the right time.

When I finished meditating, I went to the garage with renewed confidence. I repeated the same steps I had taken the night before: lifted the bags, turned them inside out and upside down and shook them. There was no sign of the key! As I was about to put the last bag back, one that I had already fully inspected, checking all of its corners, my key fell from it and dropped to the floor.

It made me chuckle. It was almost as if the message from my meditation was being confirmed: 'Let it come to you'. Had I found it in its hiding place in the bag *myself*, it would not have had the same impact. I had looked carefully but didn't see anything and yet, when I calmly folded the bag to put it away, it was unconsciously done in

such a way that the key was able to escape from its well-hidden position.
What made the experience feel so wholesome was that the ease of finding the key seemed to mirror the ease in my being. The night before, I was confident but tense as I was rushing and trying to find it with logic and will power. This time, although I had deduced that the key ought to be in one of the bags, I didn't huff and puff for a quick result. Through the message in my meditation, my hard willpower was transformed into a soft intention and I knew it was easier not to force my way into finding the key. I searched without attachment to the end result, calm and certain that I would take the right actions for the desired outcome.

It is my belief that we are invited, every moment of our lives, to act from a space of ease and trust. Only then, can we enjoy stepping into the newness of each second, interacting with life in a childlike manner, with infinite curiosity and never-ending wonder.

Free to Go

Back in 2009, my mother and I had just come back from a wonderful holiday in China. Not surprisingly, after spending 10-12 days away from home, we found our answering machine blinking. We started playing the many messages waiting for us. As we listened, I was surprised to hear two messages from my father (who didn't live with us) and one from my uncle whom I hadn't spoken to for a long time due to a family dispute. They were both urging me to call them as soon as I was back. From the tone of their voices, I knew something was wrong. But not even for a nanosecond did I consider that something could have happened to my grandfather despite his age. Pedar, as we call him – meaning father in Persian – was a strong, healthy and fit man despite being over ninety years old. At his age, he was still an inspiration, sticking to a morning exercise routine which, though naturally less demanding than in his youth, was still more than most of his peers could manage.

When I called them, they told me that Pedar was unwell and suggested that I visit him as soon as possible. Even when they gave me the name and address of the hospital where he was admitted, I wasn't alarmed. As I was driving to see him, I was comforted by his general strength and thought it was most likely a minor health issue. My other three grandparents had passed after months of grappling with illnesses and even undergoing operations, but Pedar, my last remaining grandparent, had no underlying condition and was a symbol of health. With these thoughts, reassured, I drove to the hospital.

When I arrived at 3 pm, my father was waiting outside Pedar's hospital room. He prepared me for what I was going to witness, telling me that Pedar had gone into a coma and had lost a lot of weight. I couldn't believe it, as he was absolutely fine before we headed for China. I asked my father what caused that; he said it all started with a cold, which then affected his kidneys due to an embolism and an ambulance was called. He went on to say that Pedar, who had never been admitted to the hospital, didn't want to be taken on the stretcher. He believed that if he left home horizontally, he'd never return. He wanted to sit in the ambulance and then walk into the hospital on his own two feet. The ambulance crew couldn't grant his wishes as there was a risk of him falling down and their protocol wouldn't allow him to be taken seated. Pedar had no choice but to reluctantly accept lying down. Lo and behold, as soon as he arrived, he went into a coma. I asked the doctors what could have caused his sudden decline, as I struggled to understand how his condition had worsened so severely in such a short period. Naturally, they put it down to old age and said this was not uncommon. Unfortunately, there was nothing they could do for him at this stage. My dutiful heart, as his only grandson and in fact the only one of his four grandchildren living in the country, was broken by my inability to do anything for him.

Reflecting on his life and his current circumstances, I wondered if it was selfish to want to have him back with us. In my heart of hearts, I could feel that from here on, he was only going downhill and more suffering awaited him. He had lived a good life, was healthy up to this point. Perhaps this was a moment where he could pass easily without great suffering, only if we were able to let go of him so he could be free.

We believe that while some people prefer to pass on their own, as separating from loved ones is too difficult, others wait for those dearest to them to come and say their goodbyes before leaving this world. Holding his hand, I wondered if he had waited for me, given he'd been in a coma for five days. Culturally, the son and the grandson hold a special place in the family and I sensed my unspoken duty to play my role in blessing his transition. He was the pillar of our family and I wanted to give him confidence in our ability to manage without him. I wanted him to know that, if he wanted, in case he had any doubts, he could rest peacefully. I stayed with him until 4:30 pm and before leaving, I kissed his forehead and whispered in his ear: 'If you were waiting for me, you can go now. Go to the light, if it's calling you.' With a heavy heart, I left the hospital and drove home.

As soon as I arrived, I saw a new message on the answering machine. It was my father asking me to go back as our beloved Pedar was no longer with us. My heart sank. He was gone. I was deeply sad, yet also profoundly moved. It seemed that he had indeed waited for me before he departed.

For that and a lifetime of dedication to us all, I am forever grateful. For those final moments by his side, when I felt the kindness of letting go, I am forever grateful. But, for waiting for me to say my final goodbyes, I have no words.
Both his life and his transition are a treasured gift.

Meeting in Meditation

I'm used to hearing someone say, 'I was just thinking of you' or 'I was just about to call you' when I call them. Often, I playfully claim that they must be great at sending signals that make me pick up the phone! They, on the other hand, believe I'm good at receiving. Who knows? Maybe it's a bit of both. Maybe, one day we will find out that there is an energetic corridor between us and those we know, through which we communicate without being consciously aware of it. I have heard many tell similar stories and it seems that this is a relatively common occurrence. However, what happened this time was a bit out of the ordinary.

I sat down to meditate, but as the mind often does, instead of staying focused on mantra, it took me where it wanted to go. This time, it led me to my father and we had a full-blown heart-to-heart connection. As I write this, I haven't seen him in over five years, because he lives in Iran and I'm in England. I may never see him again due to ongoing unrest in the country. So, seeing him vividly in my imagination was priceless. I could see all the details of his facial expressions, hear the tone of his voice exactly as it would be if we were sitting next to each other. Although we didn't say much, the few words we exchanged truly expressed our love and care for each other.
There was so much tenderness.

I felt immense love for him and deep compassion for the situation we found ourselves in; separated by distance with limited conversations due to his mental illness. Sadly, I find it challenging to call him more than three times a week, because each time the true distance between us, partly caused by his medication, becomes more apparent. All he says is: 'How are you? I hope you're well. I hope the family is well and your friends. I'm glad to have heard from you.' Each time, the same sentences, the same tone, no real communication, no heart-to-heart. The sadness is amplified by the fact that we used to be very close and when he was better, we had deep, meaningful and often very helpful conversations. I wouldn't have become who I am today without his gentle guidance.

Having felt his essence so vividly in my meditation, I decided to call him once I'd finished. Yet, once I got up, something else caught my attention and I didn't call him straightaway as I had planned. Five minutes later, my phone rang. When I saw his name on the caller ID, I knew he must have felt our connection. I knew this because he doesn't usually call me during that time of the day, specially on weekdays. I picked up with a big smile and a joyful heart, in contrast to the usual sadness that I feel when we talk, for what has been lost. He said, 'You called.' I chuckled and said 'Not by phone, but yes, I did call you.' I'm not sure if he followed me, but he had heard my heart, my love, loud and clear and sensed what I had experienced. He was so certain I had called him that I had to check my phone to make sure I hadn't accidentally dialled his number. I definitely hadn't made a call in the usual sense, but somehow, he'd heard my *call,* sent by the vivid, tender moments I shared with him in my imagination.

No matter how sad our circumstances seem to be, this experience showed me that our bond transcends the physical and can never be broken.

Inner Radar

I am Greek and before settling in the UK in 2008, 16 years ago, I lived in Athens. Back in 2003, I was still married to the father of my two daughters who were nine and two years old. This was a very difficult period of my life, even recalling it brings waves of sadness within me. My then-husband of 17 years showed no particular interest in our family life and had developed the habit of disappearing for a while and coming back whenever he pleased. I felt trapped between a rock and a hard place and didn't know how to free myself from the situation with two young daughters to care for.

This time, he had been gone for almost six months. I had no idea where he was or with whom, but I did know that I felt abandoned, left alone to care for our children without any support. To say that I was tired would be an understatement. Looking back, I marvel at where I found the strength to keep everything running smoothly. Not wanting my children to feel the same level of rejection that I felt, I gave them all that I had.

On that particular afternoon, I took them on my little Honda 50cc moped to a birthday party they had been invited to. Their friend's house was in Piraeus, around three miles away from our home in Drapetsona. Despite it being so close, it was not a familiar area to me as I had never needed to go there. Once I dropped them off, riding around the neighbourhood, I felt a deep knowing in my heart and mind that I would find my husband around here. It was a peculiarly strong feeling and I carried on riding with no destination in mind.

All of a sudden, without knowing why, I had the urge to pull up in front of a tall building and get off my bike. I don't remember if the door was open or if someone opened it, but I found myself climbing the stairs all the way to the last floor – I think it was the fourth. For a reason beyond my own understanding, I stood outside a flat and rang the bell. What was I doing? Anxious, I felt my heart pounding fast inside my chest as the level of adrenaline rose while I waited for someone to open the door. Who was I waiting for? It was a total mystery to me and yet, it was as if my body knew what was about to happen.

Seconds later, the door of this unknown apartment opened and I saw my husband inside. He had been living there with another woman for months. The marriage was undeniably over and I knew there was no way I could continue living that life. This strange event had saved me! Was it an angel, divine intervention, or my own subconscious guiding me to finally face reality by showing me exactly where he was and what he was up to?

Five years later, I took the bold decision to leave Greece behind and give my two beautiful daughters and myself a fresh start. That painful part of my life is over and I am now living in North London, engaged to my partner of 11 years. What happened in 2003 sparked a deep courage within me. I learned to trust that there was something inexplicable and powerful looking out for me, giving me a confidence nothing else ever could.

I would like to call it *Divine Mother* and rest in the security of knowing that she continues to show me the way, each and every day.

Going Through a Wall

As a fifteen year old lad, I remember seeing the UK premier of Pink Floyd's 'The Wall' back in 1982 at the Empire Leicester Square. I went with a good school friend and was struck not only by the production and my love for the music but the storyline and the psychic creation of the wall, which we as humans often build around ourselves.

In my twenties and having lost both parents, I started to see a wall during my meditations. It is always nice to observe phenomena with the inner eye but it wasn't long before I began to wonder. What did the wall represent? Was there a way through, over or around? One thing I knew for sure was when my wall started to go up. Early life traumas and other difficulties which accompany those years slowly darkened my skies. Once upon a time, the sunshine in any classroom or gathering, I now found solitude more comforting than being surrounded by others.

Fast forward to many years later and after having been a professional teacher for around ten years, I began to foster the idea of teaching yoga at my old school. I left that school at the end of the first sixth form, age 17, deeply traumatised and emotionally isolated. I was undergoing the stresses of watching my father slowly wither away from cancer before my eyes, along with the pressures of private school and some other demons in my life at that time.

Nearly 40 years later (around 2013) and now a successful yoga and tai chi teacher, I grew to know that I had useful skills and gifts to offer back to some of the boys attending my old school at that time. I had tried over the years to 'find my way in' but to no avail. Letter after letter, email after email, all falling on deaf ears. I even had the luck of being able to teach at the same school for girls, next door but, in my heart, I yearned to re-enter the corridors of my own past in an attempt to redeem myself from some of my *failures.* Although completely happy with my work and how this unexpected career had opened up for me like a doorway to heaven, I always had this deep itch which needed scratching. Looking back I see my ego attempting to prove itself to the world, while at the same time I think it equally important to honour the inner child who needs releasing from the trauma, frozen in past clutches of space-time.

When a dear friend passed away in 2015, my passion and interest in the practices of Lucid Dreaming & Astral Projection were rekindled. With a love and keen memory for astral and dream experiences in my childhood, which in many respects helped to steer this ship away from mainstream worldly careers and pursuits promoted by my school. My compass was always aimed at the esoteric landscape which life reminds us of when we get a little too busy with the *impermanence* of things.

I had developed a rigorous Lucid Dream & Astral Projection (OBE) program for myself. I had a daytime and nighttime practice which had been initiated back in my twenties and now rekindled in my forties. I had been reading yet another book about Astral Travel or OBE's while out and about driving for work earlier that day, followed by receiving a wonderful Thai Massage from my other half, to help with some of my body's aches and pains. I then took a delightful hot bath and did a good amount of intending.... 'Tonight I will have another OBE'. I focused with strong intent to realign with the feeling of being in the Outer Body State'. I also realigned with the intent itself. To really 'mean what I say'. This is quite often most of the work needed for many to enjoy an Out-of-Body-Experience.

So that night, I asked for assistance to experience another Out-of-Body-Experience. I had learned that asking for help can be a good thing and so I requested that my guru Sai Baba come to help me and/or send a being who could help me to 'leave my body'. This is usually referred to as 'separation', whereby the astral body moves away from the sleeping or meditator's dormant physical body. It is the astral or subtle body which gives rise to all movements of our physical form and when the physical self sleeps or the meditator is sufficiently still, s/he often begins to sense subtle waves of vibration as the astral body continues journeying with any movement or travel it may desire to make.

I began the night with some dreams about T who I grew up with and some of my school friends from my secondary school. We were all play flighting with one of the boys really going for it and over doing it a little.

I then awoke with some buzzing in my ears. If you have never had any kind of Astral Projection/OBE then you may not know that ear buzzing along with the vibratory waves (vibrational state) are common phenomena arising as preludes to an *experience*. The sound calmed down and I relaxed back towards sleep. I began to hear the buzzing again and having just pre-set the intention not to allow it to jolt me to waking state once more, it persisted beautifully.

Next thing I know, I'm having an OBE but it is happening in a dream state, which is one of the ways it can occur.

I sensed my astral body beginning to slowly move about and 'mind' cogitation of 'which way out is best?'

Then I heard the voice of the 'Gremlin'. This has been referred to by some as the 'Gatekeeper' between 'worlds', between states, between wakefulness and sleep or sleep and the next portal or dimension inwards. I had experienced this Gremlin quite a few times before. It could be considered part of an alter-ego. The renowned Don Juan Matus taught Carlos Castaneda that this voice was the Dream Emissary coming to help him dream more consciously and cross through the Seven Gates of Dreaming.

My Emissary's voice was at this time deep and ET like, sounding very much like Gollum from Lord of The Rings…

The Emissary's constant muttering brought me to increasing lucidity. I sensed my fear which is common for me as well as the excitement and then I swiftly 'buckled up!' and continued to invite the next moment to welcome me. I then felt its long hairy chimp like arms, for the first time since hearing this voice over the last couple of years. All of a sudden I was holding the creature in my arms as I floated out of my body which was lying on the bed in the lounge, with the chimp dream emissary Gollum chattering away to me. The lounge was similar to the one where I grew up.

Without looking at the Emissary, I floated out of my sleeping dream body, across the room and towards the window. As I moved the Emissary became more lifeless, like an empty puppet shell which having served its purpose, dissolved completely. It's likely that my dreaming body on the bed also dissolved as my awareness moved inwards to the next and deeper dimension.

So, when we say 'Out-of-Body-Experience', a similar expression might be that we say that we 'fall asleep'. It is perhaps more accurate to say 'Inner Body Experience' and that we, as Sylvan Muldoon so wonderfully puts it, 'Rise to sleep'.

My focus then took me floating through the glass pane of the sliding door. This would have been the door which separated my childhood lounge and the morning room extension at the back of our house. I felt the resistance of the glass as I passed through it and floated through the morning room and then out through the back windows and into what I expected to be the back garden.
Unexpectedly I was faced with darkness.

I kept floating forward slightly, fearless. This often fascinates me in Waking Reality when I recall and diarise these events, how I would expect some passings to leave me in a cold breathless sweat, while others which I fear I will fear, can be shockingly pleasant. The courage of the second body never ceases to amaze!

I approached a black wall which glistened out of the dark. It was a dark vibrating living entity.
I decided to pass through this wall-sentience before me and as I did, I also felt its gelatinous cellular viscosity. The entry seemed to trigger movement; an alien like pulsation of thick liquid black light, like visible dark matter, which oozed an abundance of cosmic life force.
It all got a little scary and I found myself automatically affirming, 'I AM THE LIGHT, I AM THE WAY' as I continued to push on through like a bold explorer!
The black mass responded,
'YOU are the light? You are the light? Youuuuu!???
Liar, Liar Knickers on Fire!
Liar, Liar Knickers on Fire!!', as an instrumental (like the Beatles' 'Sergeant Pepper's Lonely Hearts Club Band') kicked off in the background!

I felt a huge excitement sparked by the upbeat tempo and emotion and my heart expanded sending me through to the other side. A ton of grey house bricks crashed down beneath me on to the ground as I floated above them and away towards the horizon and the 'fade'. I awoke, immediately reaching for my journal.

This was a brief experience but, Energy Rich. As I wrote up my notes I felt such wondrous excitement and appreciation of life in all its multi-dimensionality.
That morning I went out to teach a yoga class and then returned home for lunch and some office work. I sat at my laptop, pulled up my old school's office email address and wrote an email.
I realised my previous errors. This time, I drafted a personal summation of my story; how I left school early, lost myself, lost myself further, lost myself completely and then decided to turn this ship around. The story flowed out of my heart painlessly and I shared how I had been blessed with love and good fortune and was now in a position to help other youngsters like my past self, who needed help.

I drafted the mail in a swift few minutes and hit the send button. I felt good. I felt really good.

I had finally said what I really wanted and needed to say. I had released what I had realised throughout the years; I was just a babe thrust in to a world of craziness and that the many traumas I had been through had scarred and moulded 'me and my' responses.

Five minutes later I received an email reply from the school office.
'Hi. This is X. M's friend from school (M is my big brother).
I have been working in the school office for the last few years now. Please come by and say hi and I'll introduce you to C and you can talk about helping us with some yoga and tai chi'.
The last time I had seen X, I was 13 years old. My parents were away, my brother threw a huge party and my great friend R (who I saw Pink Floyd's The Wall with), had been dancing on our next door neighbour's car roof after we had both drunk way too much Chartreuse Vert!

When I read the email, I knew immediately that the wall I had gone through the night before, during my OBE experience, was symbolic of my ability to go through the obstacles and barriers I had created for myself. It seemed that the many years of teaching and practicing the healing arts had indeed helped me *break through the wall.*

Echoes of the Unheard

It was a winter evening, much like any other. We were going to my father's cousin's house, who had invited us for dinner. He was an incredibly inspiring man, who had a way of lighting up a room. Strong and resilient, it was clear that he had tapped into the power of his spirit during the many years he spent in a political prison. I used to admire him, amazed at how a man could endure unimaginable torture and abuse, yet emerge with such presence. I looked forward to visiting their home whenever they invited us. Somehow, they always managed to create an ambience of cheerfulness and light through the generosity of their beings and their delicious food. Their lightness and humour were a sharp contrast to the heavy mood in the streets of Tehran, darkened by the clouds of war, scarcity and uncertainty.

That night was different, though. My father seemed restless, unable to settle. Despite the shared memories, jokes and social pleasantries, he seemed on edge. He would repeatedly get up from his seat, even during dinner, to peer out the window at our car parked nine stories below. We all secretly put his restlessness down to his bipolar symptoms. Despite our attempts to lighten the mood and assure him that the neighbourhood was safe, he couldn't shake his unease. Eventually, he excused himself to go downstairs and physically inspect the car. He took the car keys and gave a final glance outside. There he realised what had caused his inner turmoil. Our car door was open and two young men were fleeing what seemed to be their crime scene. One of them was holding in his hands what was most likely our car stereo. We all rushed down but it was too late; they were gone and so was our stereo.

Shocked, we went back up and sat around the dinner table. None of us could believe what had just happened and were totally stunned – not just by the fact that we had been robbed, but by the uncanny intuition my father had.

He had sensed them coming and knew something was wrong while the rest of us were oblivious to it. How did he know?

What is it that makes this kind of thing possible. Should we just put it down to mere coincidence and pure randomness or should we admit that there are forces at play beyond our understanding, guiding us in ways we cannot yet explain? Could it be that intuition, a higher sensitivity, or perhaps even a deep connection to the unseen allows some to perceive what lies hidden from others? Maybe they all play a part, but what is clear is that there is still a lot more to uncover in our unexplored ability to tune into the world around us.

Dancing Butterfly

When I was younger, my dad always called me Butterfly. It was a nickname that stuck and made me feel special. Needless to say, his passing left a big hole in my heart.

When planning my wedding, I knew I wanted it to be as close to my dad as possible so I chose a venue in the breathtaking Scottish Highlands, where my dad's ashes had been scattered. I wanted him to be a part of my special day, so that I could feel his presence as I stepped into the next stage of my life. I even included a photo of him in my bridal bouquet – I didn't want to go down the aisle without him by my side.

As the wedding day approached, the weather forecast was gloomy – rain, rain and more rain. This wasn't too much of a surprise, given it was the end of October. I hadn't really planned for a sun-kissed wedding. But then, on the actual day, the unexpected happened. Just for that day we were gifted with the most glorious sunshine and T-shirt weather. It was as if the universe itself conspired to bring more light and warmth to our ceremony. That was our first surprise.

Throughout the day, as I prepared for the big moment, my father was in the background of my mind. He was definitely there in spirit and I felt his presence every step of the way. And then, as I stood there, hand in hand with my husband-to-be and spoke my vows, it happened: A butterfly, delicate and beautiful, fluttered into the castle and flew straight towards us as if guided by the heavens. It then danced around us for what felt like an eternity. It was magnificent to watch, as though it were showering us with blessings. I felt a warmth, a presence, a connection that I couldn't quite explain. It was as if my dad had sent this sublime messenger to tell me that he was with me – his Butterfly. I sensed that it was his way of showing his approval and that he was also sharing this special moment with us.

The rest of the day was filled with love and laughter as we enjoyed a late summer's day in October! Needless to say, the weather returned to its typical Scottish ways – pouring down with rain the following day.

This wasn't the first time my dad had reached out to me from the beyond, but it certainly was the most touching. Usually, he comes to me in dreams and gives me advice and guidance. But on this day, in that old castle in the highlands, he sent a butterfly to dance with us, bless our union and remind me that he would always be a part of my life, no matter what.

Opera

One day, out of the blue, I felt like going to see an opera, which was really random for me. Even though I enjoy opera, it's not something I'd go out of my way to see. On the odd occasion I felt like seeing one, I'd usually just watch a DVD or find one online. But this time was different; I had an unusually strong feeling, almost a craving, to go out and see an opera specifically. I wasn't able to act on it at the time, but it stayed on my mind to book a ticket as soon as I could.

Fast forward a couple of weeks, around my birthday, a friend sent me a text saying: 'I have a surprise for you. Meet me at Covent Garden station at X o'clock and make sure you're not late. It's really important!' Luckily, I was able to make it on time and was overjoyed to find out what the surprise was: she had booked us to see an opera, not a play, but an opera.

How could I explain this? Was it that she'd already booked the opera and I somehow sensed it? Or had she unconsciously picked up on my sudden desire to go? Either I tuned into her intention, or she sensed mine. Regardless, the experience brought a special depth to my birthday treat infusing it with a sense of wonder and mystery.

For someone else, this may seem like a random and meaningless coincidence, which is understandable. Yet for me, it was a true *wow* moment, unexpected and somehow sacred. It is through moments like this that I am reminded of the aliveness and richness of what lies beneath the surface of the ordinary. This helps me move along my path with more clarity and trust, even when I can't see where it leads.

Wrong Turn

I was about to leave the house to go to a friend's place – she had invited me and a few other girlfriends for dinner, when I realised I might be running a few minutes late. I find that so embarrassing! Knowing that the host would have spent the entire day preparing for a great evening, the least I could do as a guest, was to show some respect and turn up on time. Unfortunately, it looked like I was going to let the host down this evening.

Still, I didn't want to arrive all flustered and stressed, so instead of putting my foot down and driving like a madwoman, I decided to chant. I chose to breathe out the sound of 'aaah' – believed to help manifest our desires. According to Tibetan traditions, it strengthens the power of our vision and helps us effortlessly bring what we have in mind into the world. I decided to put it to test again but this time for a small wish: arriving on time. I had already witnessed some amazing and unexpected results before, including manifesting unlikely solutions to more serious problems. As I chanted in the car, I visualised myself arriving on time or at least not uncomfortably late. It is perhaps worth mentioning that vocalising the breath like chanting 'aaah', extends the exhalations, which in turn has a very relaxing effect on the entire nervous system. By chanting aaah, I was killing two birds with one stone: Giving myself the chance to stay calm and relaxed, while doing the only thing I could do, at the time, to potentially save myself from the embarrassment of arriving late.

Deep in my practice, I arrived at a roundabout where I usually take the first exit towards my friend's. In the thickness of the fog, that exit seemed to have disappeared and I failed to see it. By the time I realised, it was too late. I had no choice but to try and take a left turn into an off road to rejoin the main road I had missed. Unfortunately and to my disbelief, all the roads that would lead to it were closed due to some roadworks.

I felt really annoyed with myself for missing an exit that I had taken so many times before. As natural as it was to indulge in the feeling of frustration, I decided to go with the flow instead. I didn't have much choice anyway and nothing good would come out of my resistance. To help myself and shake these feelings off, I resumed my chanting.

By the time I arrived, I had regained my inner equilibrium and even though I was slightly late, I didn't feel as uncomfortable as I'd thought I'd be. The breathing – chanting – had done its magic. As chance would have it, I was actually amongst the first guests. When I apologised and explained the reason for my lateness to the host, she told me how lucky I had been not to take that exit at the roundabout. It would have led me to the main road where the traffic would have been horrendous due to major roadworks. That explained why the side roads were all closed! She told me that she hadn't realistically expected anyone arriving on time and the other guests trickled in, all delayed by the heavy traffic. So, it turned out after all, the best route I could've taken to her house that evening, was the one that I had *accidentally* taken.

I wonder if deeply relaxing in myself, I'd opened myself up to a *knowing* that would otherwise be veiled. But, I didn't know not to take the exit, it was momentarily hidden from my awareness to stop me from taking it. My mind wants a logical answer but I don't have one. I'm only left with a quiet sense of awe.

After an experience like this, it's hard for me to see frustrating and annoying events in the same light. There is now, always, an underlying belief that what appears to be a *detour* may actually be exactly what is needed to put us onto - or back to – the right track.

Calls to the Universe

In July 2017, I travelled from London to Dorset for a 3-day yoga workshop to immerse myself in the yogic vibes and deepen my understanding of the physical aspects of yoga. It was a magical long weekend; I was in my element, as for me, studying is undeniably one of life's most cherished luxuries. I made a few friends with whom I had partnered and shared notes during our engaging sessions. At the end of the second day, when the workshop ended at 5:30 pm, five of us set off to the bank of a nearby river to take advantage of the long, glorious summer day. It's fascinating what two days of yoga practice, where the body continually sheds tension, can do. We become more receptive to the little joys of life and obstacles to intimacy also vanish. Bonding and connecting deeply with others on the journey becomes as natural as it once was in the innocence of childhood.

We merrily walked towards the riverbank and when we arrived, we spread a cosy blanket on the ground and settled in for some heartfelt chit-chat. We were all pretty upbeat; this was after all a learning holiday, a break away from our everyday routine and obligations. Without making a formal decision, we were drawn to chant and meditate as we were far enough from the path to avoid strange glances. After a while, I shared with them how conscious I had become of all the physical, emotional and mental tension carried in the voice as we talk or sing. I had come to see that, without realising it, many of us block the breath and stop the natural voice from being expressed. I explained that I was re-learning how to speak or chant while staying open to my breath.

My passion for the subject seemed contagious and we decided to do an exercise that I had recently learned from a book by Barefoot Doctor – *The Urban Warrior*. In order to avoid complaints from neighbours, he advises going out to a wood or a park and pretending to call our dog. The goal of this practice is to let the breath fly out as we shout a name in order to allow the breathing muscles to work, release stress and open up. The idea is that adults rarely use the full potential volume of their voice – hence the power of their breath – compared to children. Overtime, this can lead to atrophy of the breathing muscles as they are not used to their full capacity. Barefoot Doctor suggests calling the dog Riley, but obviously we can call our imaginary dog any name we choose. Everyone seemed enthusiastic to practice this to feel the results. So we started. Four of us chose the name Riley and one lady chose Rover. So, there we were, letting the sounds fly out as we called out to our imaginary dogs. It was a blast and we had a good laugh afterwards (also good for the breathing muscles!).

After a while, we decided to walk back to town as we had another full day of study ahead of us. Fifteen minutes into our walk up a steep hill, a beautiful dog ran playfully towards us and greeted us warmly. His owner, a lady in her 40s, told us how friendly and sociable her dog was. To show more interest in her furry companion, I asked what his name was. 'Roley', she replied! Roley? We'd just been calling out to Rover and Riley and now a dog named Roley comes to greet us?

Was the universe teasing us? Had we been played or had we somehow manifested Roley out of thin air by calling our imaginary dogs? We were all gobsmacked and couldn't believe this extraordinary coincidence. We laughed in utter surprise, but under the apparent lightheartedness, deep questions were brewing:
Is there more to us than we understand?
Can we really think of something, connect to it and then see it come to life?
Can our intention shape our reality?

The possibility that we may one day find answers to questions like these and explain such phenomena, enlivens my soul.

Am I or Aren't I?

I grew up in a wonderful family with one elder brother in a loving home. I was born in 1967 and brought up Jewish, with my father being a South African Jew of Russian descent and my mother an Irish Jew from Dublin. What's that? An Irish Jew and of what descent? This is the response I would get, whenever I would share my family's roots.

Thus, from a very early age my mother had instilled the existence of the Dublin community within us, preparing us for the onslaught of questions that would arise over the years. Indeed as I grew up, my friends' parents would always ask, 'So where are your parents from?' Many of them were astonished to hear of 'Irish Jews' and so, as a young boy, I was able to educate them. I must say looking back, that still feels good: Ireland's Jewish history began around 1,000 years ago with the first synagogue being built around 1660. The population gradually expanded from 258 in 1871 to nearly 5,000 in 1904 (Wikipedia) and has now declined to about half of that.

My mother had been widowed shortly before my brother was born and soon remarried and had me. My half brother has always been my whole brother. When we were young we were very close and although we now live our own lives, there remains a true and deep love between us.

From as far back as I can remember (cot, pram, that far), we used to visit my Ma's in-laws (from her first marriage), at least a couple of times a year. They lived in Stamford Hill, London and for me they were *our* grandparents. When we went to visit Uncle Stanley his two sisters Thelma and Phyllis were usually there.

We went to a Catholic state primary school which I absolutely loved and also went to synagogue every Saturday morning, belonging to the Reform community. We attended Hebrew school on Sundays from the age of about six until Bar Mitzvah at 13. I continued until I was 15.

This all went out of the window when I felt the pressure of secondary school and the looming of exams. I haven't been back to 'shul' (synagogue) since, except for the odd wedding over the years and more commonly to the burial grounds for funerals.

Over all of those years growing up, I sometimes wondered why I seemed to be just as fond of Jesus and Christmas as I was of Esther and Purim or the Angel of Death and Passover. I could also never quite forget the disapproving face of one of my friends' parents who had great difficulty in digesting the fact that some Jews lived over the water in Ireland. They just didn't wish to believe this could be true.

My parents passed away pretty early, when they were 62; my father in 1988 and my mother in 1995. God rest both their souls. When my Ma left her body in 1995 it struck me like lightning that I was an orphan. My mother had requested to be cremated which although now is not uncommon within the faith, is certainly not the norm. We had discussed this while she was alive and I had agreed with her that I too would like to go the same way. I was aware back then that Hindus like to rise upwards towards their soul and had always felt it lighter and easier when watching a film – to see the flames climbing towards the ethers than the tears falling in to a deep hole in the ground.

The ceremony at the Finchley Crematory Grounds was heavily attended by so many loving faces. All was a blur of images morphing in and out of my tears. I was traumatised and didn't know it. We returned to my family home for prayers and my mothers' elder sister, younger brother and niece from Dublin all attended. It was then that the weirdness started.

I realised that my uncle was pretty intoxicated and the condolence card and flowers they handed us were really out of sorts. One card even had a crucifix on it, so the seed of enquiry which the doubting parents had planted years before, began to sprout a little more. The moment was surreal, as my brother and I stood in the garden talking to our Irish relatives. They were the furthest thing from 'Jewish' imaginable.

In my late twenties, in response to questioning the unconscious about my mother's true religious identity – two or three years after she had passed, I had an out-of-body-experience (something I was deeply into then and still am). To this date, it remains one of the most potent, mystical and beyond body ecstatic experiences I have had.

I was led from one dream which I do not recall, into the OBE.
I was standing in a smallish rectangular room with my mother. All was more real than real.
She was glowing white purity and radiating deep ecstatic peace.
The room vibrated with holiness. Not religiousness but divine bliss that words cannot reach.
My mother led me towards the middle of the room whereby stood a glass container, the same manner of which you will find in any museum and which is secure enough to protect God's law. Inside, without apparent mount, stood a Magen David – the Star of David – a luminous pulsation of vibrating God matter, about the size of a skull. The vibration filled the room like a silent big bang of unconditional love and the light filled my mind until so bright I have no recall of the next moment. I am not sure if I awoke immediately or moved back into the dream state. When I did surface to the waking state, I was of course greatly moved. Not only had my dream, my mother's spirit and what felt like God, answered my prayer – I had also enjoyed a life changing experience. Up to that point I felt satisfied. My mother was a Jew and lived and died a Jewish life. I returned to the ups and downs of life, feeling the uncertainty finally behind me.

Many years later, after I met and had been living with my wife for a few years, as is normal, family stories are exchanged and memories aroused. I told her the story of the doubts my brother and self had experienced regarding my mother's religious past. Through chatting it became clear that I should reach out to some of my family, now that Facebook was a thing. Perhaps lost contacts could be re-established. After very little effort, we found my South African cousins, one still there and the other living in Canada. That was it. There was nothing on my mother's side from the Emerald Isle. Perhaps I didn't look hard enough but we left it there.

It wasn't until around 2012 that I started to wonder if my mother's former in-laws, who once lived in Stamford Hill, might still be alive. I was keen to make some contact. Perhaps if I was really lucky, I might be able to ask some questions about the story of their late brother. Maybe they could give me more details on how he had eloped with my mother and left Dublin to marry in London, madly and deeply in love. I knew the internet had exhausted its wisdom and so I sent out a prayer into the sky one day while I was driving between High Barnet and Borehamwood.

I asked God: 'If Uncle Stanley or Auntie Thelma or Phyllis are still around, please help me to find them'.

The following month I received a phone call. At the time we were doing some work with Age UK and taught senior sessions for them in some of their care homes around the area. I was asked to come to teach a group at the Borehamwood site. Off I went and arrived into a room attended by about 20 seniors. Amongst the group of ladies and gents, there were some who were very withdrawn and feeble. Their faces were empty or very stern with grey wrinkles which clung to the ground like stone. Naturally I felt relieved and welcomed by the rare few with eyes like crystals and a history of lines many of which arced towards the sky. We had fun. I taught the hour's session and as was the norm, the banter and humour arose with the aches and groans as the odd cussing and group dynamic electrified the room. What a laugh!

Right from near the beginning of the session I clicked in with a gentleman straight in front of me and towards the back of the room. He had a Liverpudlian accent with a hint of something even more familiar. At the end of the session I was drawn towards him to chat. In hindsight, I see how easily I could have just upped it and left the room beaming.

I stood by him and said 'Hi, where are you from?'
'Liverpool' he replied, 'but originally from Dublin.'
'Oh' I said 'My mum was a Dubliner.'
'From which part did she come?' he asked.
'Unfortunately I never knew' I said. 'From somewhere outside the centre, towards the sticks.'
'What was her name?' he said.
'Jackie. Jackie Cully' I replied.
'Oh Jackie!' he burst, 'she married Maurice, she converted, Stanley is my best friend' (referring to Uncle Stanley).
My body stood quite still!
My spirit was knocked to the back of the room in disbelief!
For a few moments I just reeled in the seemingly impossible which had just revealed itself.
The gentleman took out his mobile phone and gave me my uncle's telephone number.

And so it was. I needed no more proof.

I did of course call my uncle who told me the story of how my mother had gone to the ends of the world and back to become an orthodox jew. He said 'She did it properly, she really did', to which my eyes still well up today.

What were the odds of that? I wanted to know if my mother's in-laws were still around and asked to find them. A few weeks later, I found myself teaching someone I had never met before who happened to know them. Just like that, he led me straight to them and the answer to a lifelong question that held part of my identity was finally revealed.

Pregnancy

My brother and I shared a special bond and had a lot in common. Before he started a family of his own, we would speak regularly and talk about anything and everything. Our conversations were always filled with childlike joy and laughter. When we were together, we weren't grown-ups; the playful brother and sister would come alive, curious about everything and ready to explore.

Whenever I called him, he'd playfully say, 'I concentrated hard for you to call me. It must have been the power of my mind that made you pick up the phone!' *Mind power* was the subject of many of our conversations and the last time I saw him, I remember giving him '*The Silva Mind Control Method*' book by José Silva.

Sadly, on Boxing Day, 26 December 2020, his heart stopped and he left us forever. Already overwhelmed by the emotional turbulence of the pandemic and lockdown, his passing was truly devastating. The terrible news arrived when everyone in our household had Covid and as if things couldn't get any worse, my husband was hospitalised a few days later. He came close to passing to the other side too, but thankfully, he miraculously recovered and returned home to us. That period was beyond intense. It wiped us out like a tornado.

Naturally, the months that followed were clouded by grief. I hadn't just lost a brother; I had lost my close friend. I longed to see him and talk to him in my dreams. I couldn't believe he was gone and was convinced he was still with us and would eventually make his presence known and communicate with us – somehow. On the surface everything was the same. I carried on as though nothing had happened – going through the motions – but inside I felt lifeless.

Fast forward to a year later, my daughter, a dentist who had recently married the man of her dreams, decided to return to university for another three years to specialise in gum disease. She had made a firm decision to wait until after her studies to start a family.

Before my daughter completed her enrolment for the course, I finally dreamt of my beloved brother. In the dream, he stood in front of my daughter and me and gave us the news that she was pregnant and would have her child sooner than expected. I took his message on board as if I knew not to deny or resist it. When I woke up, the dream had slipped my mind completely. Shortly after, my daughter called me. I could hear that she was worried so I asked what was troubling her. She said that she was late and suspected she might be pregnant. As soon as she uttered those words, I remembered my dream. Completely blown away, I said that my brother had already told me in the dream that she was pregnant. She couldn't believe it. Knowing that my brother had brought us the news inspired her and boosted her with confidence. Her tone changed and I sensed she was relieved of any anxiety around the possibility of starting a family sooner than she'd planned. She excitedly agreed to call me as soon as she had the results from the test.

When she later confirmed my brother's message, I was speechless. Somehow, he had found a way to communicate with me from wherever he was, giving me the wonderful news that a beautiful soul was on its way to our family. My precious granddaughter is now six months old and has brought us hope, joy and much-needed laughter!

He's not here to hold her in his arms, but he knew she was coming before any of us. That alone is enough to show me our connection will never die.

Which Car?

I had never been into cars. For me, a car was a means of transportation that would take me from point A to point B. My ex-husband was the one who would choose and buy our cars. He seemed to know what to look for and would always explain the reasoning behind his choices. I was always convinced, not because I understood what he was talking about, but because I trusted him implicitly and had no desire to learn anything about cars myself.

The first time I had to buy my own car after my divorce, I found the task so daunting that I asked my partner to choose it for me. We saw an advert, went to see the car, liked it and bought it there and then. It was straightforward – no fuss, no weighing up too many options! My partner said it was a good car and I took his word for it. This little green Renault Clio turned out to be a hassle-free and reliable car that drove me around for years.

I had been driving it for about five or six years when an acquaintance reproached me for not ditching this now-old car for a newer, more stylish one. I knew that for him, status and cars went hand in hand. His underlying belief was: the better or more expensive a car, the more likely its owner was successful. I didn't subscribe to this mentality and I had a different definition of success. I felt free and wonderful driving the same car for years, even though it represented no status and was considered an average car. After many years of driving it, the sense of familiarity felt very much like a close friendship! This unimpressive car had seen my tears, my laughter, my dance and heard me sing at the top of my voice! (Poor thing!) She knew all my moods and was there for me when I needed her. Yes, my car had become my friend and I was not going to change it to upgrade my *apparent* status.

However, when the time did come to choose another car, for the first time, I decided to do it my way. I wanted to choose it myself and be the one to decide which attributes mattered to me. Apart from reliability and freedom of movement, I had no idea what to look for. As I looked around, I realised that, in truth, there were not many cars on the market that I liked. The only one that I would choose for its cute shape was the new Beetle. Unfortunately, even though it was apparently a good choice mechanically, it wasn't a good choice financially. A second-hand Beetle, I soon found out, was £20,000 so given my budget of £5000, I let go of the idea. For the next couple of years, I researched and test-drove many cars, but none pulled my heartstrings.

I was starting to get desperate, as my Renault Clio was showing more signs of ageing and I knew I had to make a decision quickly. My partner and I decided to go to a large second-hand car supermarket to increase our chances. As we were about to leave the house, my daughter shouted from her bedroom: '
Mum, get a black car with cream leather inside.'
'Sure,' I said, 'wish me good luck!'

When we arrived there, I was pleasantly surprised at the range of cars that were available. As we were walking around, checking different ones, I saw a few Beetles in a far corner. I knew they were beyond my budget, but I was still pulled their way. I couldn't believe my eyes when I saw a cute little black Beetle with cream leather inside.
I wanted it!
But, even with the massive price drop in the last couple of years, it was still 60% over my set budget. I couldn't deny the sign, though! 'A black car with cream leather,' she had shouted! Did she know I was going to be tempted and was giving me the push to go for what we both wanted? I wanted her to be happy with my choice and I really wanted a Beetle, so I convinced myself that her words were meant for me. They were an invitation to be less frugal and let go of being over-prudent. So, I decided to treat myself to what I had wanted all along and spend the £8000 joyfully. This purchase wasn't going to put me in debt, after all!

Khaleh Souskeh – named after a Persian story character – meaning black beetle, was a true friend! She was my daughter's practice car after she passed her driving test and wore her resulting bumps and scars proudly. She rescued my partner, whose job depended on being mobile on many occasions, when his car was being fixed. Not once did she let me down in 16 years. As hard as it was to let her go, I delight in the story of how she came to us as if it was meant to be. Would I have made the same decision without my daughter's nudge? Who knows?

Entry Exam

I finished high school in 1988 in Tehran, shortly after the Iran-Iraq war ended. I wanted to continue my education and become a pharmacist, fully aware that this was no simple task. The country was still dealing with the impact of the war and there were very few spaces at universities. To get into one of my chosen state universities meant going through a daunting national entry exam that was hours long and required much preparation. The stress around this exam was unbelievable! We regularly heard acquaintances who had mental or emotional breakdowns as they prepared for or failed it. My first attempt, despite many sleepless nights and hours of studying, wasn't successful. I knew I had to spend another year of hard work and retake it. For me, this was the only choice as the other option – applying to private universities, which were few and far between and did not have the same reputation or calibre as state ones – was not appealing.

During the war, all universities were closed for four years and high school graduates of that period had no choice but to prepare for the day they could take the exam. This created a significant backlog of students striving to enter university, making the competition extremely high. To put it in perspective, approximately 3,000,000 students would sit the exam, but only 2000 would succeed in securing a university place for any given subject. With priority given to men the ratio of success was 60% male versus 40% female. This meant I had to work much harder as a woman if I were to pursue higher education. To complicate matters further, there was another rule which worked against me: anyone who had lost a family member in the war would automatically receive favourable consideration, making their chances of success *three times* higher.

Looking back, the pressure of the national entry exam was unusually high. If successful, the names of those who passed, as well as the subject and university, would be published in the national newspaper getting the whole country buzzing with the news. It was a big achievement to overcome all the barriers and succeed. The exam itself was unbelievably stressful. Unlike here in America, where I currently live and work as a pharmacist, we couldn't just study the subjects relevant to our degree. In Iran, we were tested on all the subjects we had studied during our four years of high school: that's 14 subjects to A-level standard. *(In the West, our high school diploma is generally undervalued: the West tends to consider the equivalent qualification as being at a much lower level. Perhaps due to perceptions of Iran as a developing nation.)*

To increase their chances of success, those who could afford it attended private classes after school. This was not only to deepen the knowledge of their subjects but also to learn and prepare for the exam's format. I was fortunate in that regard and was able to have the extra support. Having said that, there was no way of escaping the long hours of dedicated studies.

A few days before the exam day, I started experiencing brain fog. Clearly I had studied and revised to the limits of my brain's capacity. I would pick up a book, look at it, attempt to read it, but nothing would stick. There was no way I could cram in the less important subjects that I had neglected in the past few months. I wasn't able to shake this off and on the night before the exam, I knew it was too late! Although I was fully aware that there was no way this exam could be postponed, I secretly prayed for a miracle.

The next day, I woke up to the breaking news across the country. Ayatollah Khomeini, the leader of the Islamic Republic of Iran, had passed away and the country was declared in a state of mourning.

I had no death wish on him or anyone else, but as fate would have it, the national exam was postponed and I was given a second chance to revise.

As naive as it may seem to believe that the universe responded to my personal pleas, I cannot deny that it certainly felt that I was supported towards my dreams. Without the extra time the door to success wouldn't have opened and I would not be admitted at my chosen university in 1989.

A Nudge in a Dream

We rented a flat in a beautiful area of Hertfordshire, surrounded by stunning old houses and mansions that gave it a distinct charm. It was a dream location, within walking distance to beautiful woods. We couldn't believe our luck when we found a reasonably priced flat in such a sought-after neighbourhood. The downside was that the mere mention of the location and postcode would make people assume that we belonged to the millionaires' club. Though we were fortunate in many ways, we certainly didn't have the same financial power as our neighbours, including our landlord, who lived in the grand mansion next to our two-bedroom flat.

Our landlords, a pleasant and easy-going couple, were generally friendly. But when it came to spending money on repairs for their old flat, unless very urgent, we could always feel their strong resistance. To some extent, this was understandable. Who enjoys receiving calls from tenants reporting issues that need fixing? On one occasion, though, their shrewdness went too far. They attempted to make us pay for a pre-existing leak that had affected the neighbour below us for years. It was intermittent and had started at least ten years before we moved in. Had the lovely gentleman downstairs not shared this information, we would have accepted the landlord's suggestion that we had caused the leak and would have been faced with a huge bill. I found it hard to accept that such an affluent person would be willing to put the blame on us, knowing full well that this had been going on for years. Thankfully, we were able to avoid falling into this financial trap.

Given the age of the house, it wasn't uncommon for something to go wrong at least once a year. On this particular occasion, I had texted our landlord about a new problem. I believe it was to do with our boiler. He had promised to get back to me as soon as possible. But a week passed and I heard nothing back. Reluctantly, I texted him again and another week went by without a response. I could feel my impatience and frustration rise with each passing day, but I didn't want to pester him, knowing he was aware of the issue. One morning, just before waking, I had a dream – a clear sign that my annoyance had reached its limits.

In this dream, I found myself scolding our landlord in the same way a mother would her child. I was shouting at him in disappointment:
'When will you become rich?
Why are you being so miserly and frugal?
How much money do you need to feel abundant?'
I even told him off for his obsession with preserving his Aston Martin, which he carefully stored in a garage and only drove once a month to avoid adding mileage.

My dream was interrupted by my alarm just after I yelled: 'Be rich and stop acting so poor!'

What a relief it was to wake up from such an emotionally charged situation. I picked up my phone to stop the alarm and to my utter surprise, a text arrived there and then. It was from my landlord, the message read: 'When will you be available? I am sending someone over to check the issue.' He might as well have said: 'I've heard you, I am rich and abundant enough to send someone to fix this problem.'

In that moment, the dream and waking reality seemed to have merged and I was flabbergasted at the possibility of having communicated my disapproval of him in a different dimension. A mere coincidence? It might have been, but it certainly felt as though he had heard me loud and clear and responded accordingly.

Finding Myself

It was the end of summer 2014 when my cousin ended up in hospital in Cyprus, undergoing chemotherapy to fight a recurrence of cancer. Although I live in London, our bond was incredibly strong and I felt a powerful urge to be by her side. I wanted to be there for her and my aunt, so I flew there as soon as I could. When I arrived I realised that her condition was irreversible and there was no hope that one day, she would be able to sing, dance and live her full artist's life. My heart ached to see a mother helplessly watch her child's body slowly failing. It all seemed terribly unfair and cruel!

Deep down, I think that my cousin knew her suffering and gradual decline was the only way her family would be able to let her go. I was with them during the final three weeks of her life, witnessing her parents' pain as they sought to bring her some peace. She had endured far too much suffering and as much as they loved her, they knew they had to surrender to the inevitable.

This period played a crucial role in my own journey and I deeply reflected on life and the point of it all. I had realised firsthand that everything can be snatched away in an instant.
I will never forget my dying cousin's words to her mother:

'Live your life.'

Her words echoed in my mind for the months that followed.

When I returned to the UK, I was overwhelmed by an inner chaos. Grieving emotions consumed me and I didn't feel I belonged anywhere, not even with those close to me. I was not my usual self and couldn't go back to who I used to be either.
I needed to pause and give myself time to reflect.
I had to find myself!

Asia was calling me! I had a strong urge to travel there on my own, so I made the decision to go. I loosely planned to visit a yoga retreat, hoping it would help me find some inner peace.

One evening, as I gazed up at the sky, I had a sense that something special was about to happen. Not knowing what to expect, I promised myself to say *yes* if it felt right and to follow whatever resonated with me during my travels. This time, I was determined to prioritise my own needs. In the past, I had struggled to do that, often caring for others even to my own detriment. Now, I embraced this new resolve with enthusiasm: 'Live your life.'

I began my journey in North Thailand and explored several breathtaking destinations. However, after a motorbike accident that left me with an injured knee, I decided to move on, so I went to a travel agency to find my next destination. They gave me two flight options: one to Koh Lanta and the other to Koh Phangan. As I preferred to arrive during the daytime, the decision was made and I chose Koh Phangan.

It was there that I celebrated Christmas at a lively beach party where I met a warm and friendly group of Portuguese people. They kindly invited me to join them the next day to a festival I was already planning to attend on New Year's eve. Plus, I had already booked my boat ticket to spend some time on an island the next day. So, I politely declined. One of the Portuguese men said, 'Are you crazy? Why are you going alone? Take my number and call me if you change your mind.'

The following morning, while waiting to board the boat, a sudden storm hit us. The atmosphere very quickly became chaotic and all the other passengers and I sought shelter. Drenched, squashed and anxious, I reached for my ticket only to realise that I had lost it. Faced with this dilemma, I whispered to the universe, 'If I don't find my ticket, I'll take it as a sign to contact the Portuguese man from the party and go to the festival with them.'

My ticket was nowhere to be found, it must have dropped in the frenzy of finding shelter from the pouring rain. So, I called him. He immediately came to my rescue and brought me to where he was staying with his friends – a yoga teacher and a hula hoop performer. There they were, two people who shared the same passion for my two most favourite activities. I stayed with them and the next day, another one of their friends – Tony – joined us. We all had an unforgettable time at the festival and I felt as though I had known these guys all my life.

Little did I know that a strong storm and a lost ticket – seemingly unfortunate events – would lead to my magical romantic story. Had it not been for these circumstances, I would not have been led to find Tony, who later became my husband and the father of our son.

This experience has radically changed my perception of so-called *bad* events. To this day, whenever I lose something or find myself in an uncomfortable or weary place, I remember that:

The difficulties that come my way, may be the keys to more opportunities.

Stranger in London

I have been divorced for about 17 years and am lucky to have two wonderful children, a girl and a boy. The three of us shared a special bond, with my daughter and I being particularly close. Compared to my children's upbringing, mine was shaped by traditional Islamic values and parents who were strict and distrustful. I wanted to give them a different experience growing up, one that would allow them the freedom to experience life their way, while knowing they could always count on my unwavering support.

This wasn't an easy path given our culture. I am from Turkey and my ex-husband is from Pakistan. Despite his and other family members' disagreements, I stood firm in my approach. In my view, maintaining a strong bond with my children while giving them healthy guidance would work a lot better than strict parenting. I knew that if they were determined to do something, they would find a way, whether secretly or not. Through honesty and openness, I was able to enter their world and support them when needed.

I valued and cherished our relationship which was built on mutual trust and understanding.

When my daughter was at university, in 2019, I noticed a change in her behaviour which alarmed me. She was working two jobs and receiving grants for her university, yet she always seemed short of money. I knew she enjoyed going out, clubbing and dancing; still, the situation made me suspicious. Whenever I questioned her about it, she would become defensive and dismissive, not her typical behaviour. I was losing her. We used to share everything with each other, without being careful about what was said, but now, she was distant and reluctant to confide in me. I knew something wasn't right.

Then, one day while tidying her room, I came across a letter from the bank giving her notice that a fraud investigation had started. I was shocked and deeply worried. I didn't know how to approach her knowing how secretive she'd been. Despite the seriousness of this situation, she'd kept everything to herself. I felt truly inadequate as a parent, not knowing how to reach her.

A short while before this, she had introduced me to this young man that she was seeing. From the moment I met him, I had a bad feeling and told her the truth. I knew that my concerns wouldn't be pleasant, so I tried to be as tactful as I could. I expressed my reservations about him, but couldn't explain the reason. After finding the letter, I knew I had to get her to open up to me. This was too serious a matter for her to face alone. So I made the tough decision to do something I had never done before: I lied. I fabricated a story and told her that the police had contacted me about a fraud investigation at our address. I told her that I knew it wasn't me or her brother as he was too good a citizen to do anything of that nature. My obvious anguish and the story were convincing enough for her to come clean.

She started sharing the horrifying truth about the boy she was seeing. He was physically, emotionally and mentally abusive to her. As part of a grooming gang he was exploiting her, taking all her hard-earned money, even making her take loans from dangerous loan sharks. She confessed that she was now in a lot of debt.

In that moment, my world literally turned upside down. Throughout the years, my main priority had been to protect my children and shield them from all painful experiences. I had done my absolute best to create an open environment at home and yet, she had suffered in silence without me by her side.

Though the news hit me hard, I knew I couldn't break down. My maternal instinct kicked in and the warrior mother inside emerged, ready to take on any challenge. I promised to shield her from any more harm and not stop until I resolved this issue.

I had a friend who was working for the police at the time. I rang her and asked what I should do. She told me that my daughter should go straight to the police station and report him. When I shared this with her, I witnessed a scene that I will never, ever forget. She started trembling, crying and hiding herself behind a door. What had happened to my beautiful girl? Where was I when she needed me? I blamed myself for having given them too rosy an outlook on life. I had done her wrong by teaching her to see the best in people and their good intentions until proven otherwise. She clearly hadn't been able to see the signs before the situation had held her captive.

She was clearly terrified of him. It turned out he had made horrific threats to kill her and her brother, claiming he knew which university he attended. He even threatened to have me raped and murdered in the most hideous ways and the list went on… Her fear was not for herself, but for us – her family. I reassured her again that I would not allow anyone or anything to harm us. I managed to convince her to gather her courage and report the abuse and threats to the police. Once she did, they brought him in for questioning, but due to a lack of concrete evidence, they couldn't do anything. They had to release him. Her fear skyrocketed once she heard the news. She felt too unsafe to stay at home. So we spent the following weeks going to hotel rooms, staying with friends and even travelled abroad. Spain gave us a chance to get some much-needed sleep and clarity.

Obviously, we couldn't stay there forever. When we came back from Spain, we made a conscious decision to choose courage over living in constant fear of threats. We couldn't continue our lives like fugitives, running away from our own home. The police were extremely helpful, sending patrol units to our area whenever we were worried. They even gave us a priority line, which meant they would come to us quicker than usual should the need arise. This gave me a relative sense of security, but not enough for me to sleep peacefully through the nights. Every slight noise or passing car would wake me up in panic. I had chosen courage, yet deep down, I was petrified.

One early morning, when my daughter was returning home at 2 am after a late shift at the supermarket, she was confronted by a group of guys in a car. They cut her off and stopped her car, saying that they were sent by her ex-boyfriend who wanted to see her. She immediately called me and without delay we contacted the police. Once again, without evidence, nothing could be done. There was no actual threat coming directly from him. We were helplessly stuck in this never-ending cycle of fear and vulnerability.

I lost my zest for life, feeling depressed and anxious all the time. The weight of this burden was so heavy that I began to question everything – my way of life, my beliefs and my values. Despite always having a strong faith in God, I found myself questioning his intentions and even his existence. During one of my lowest points, I was sitting in front of my meditation table consumed with raw emotions, so I cried out to God: 'Do you even exist? Who have I been praying to all these years? If you are real, where are you now? You know how unjust and horrible this situation is. Where is your support? I am losing my faith in you and I fear that all my beliefs were based on lies.' I will never forget the rawness of this plea that poured out from the depth of my pain.

A few days passed. We went to a café in London to celebrate my ex-husband's birthday. We don't often go to London, but it was a special occasion and he had wished for the four of us to eat there. After the meal, we strolled to an ice cream place.

I'm not usually one to initiate conversations with strangers, as I tend to be quite reserved. However, on that day, unlike my usual self, I started a conversation with a lady who had just sat at the table next to us. I asked her, 'Has the rain stopped?' and she replied, 'Not quite.' We carried on with some small talk about the weather and it became clear that she was also Turkish. Not only had I started talking to her, which was out of character for me, I found myself prying into her private life too. I surprised myself when I asked, 'What do you do?' to which she responded, 'I teach Taekwondo.' I didn't expect that answer as she was so stunning that I would have found it more believable if she'd said that she was a model. Curious, I asked her how she got into Taekwondo. She replied, 'Well, my reasons were personal.'

She opened up more and revealed that she had been a victim of severe abuse until she made the radical decision never to let anyone physically harm her again, which is why she took up Taekwondo. As she shared more details, I learned that her ex-boyfriend was from the same country as my daughter's. Her story was incredibly inspiring and I felt compelled to ask if she would be willing to take my daughter on as a student. I thought this could help her rebuild her confidence and give her the ability to protect herself. The lady sensed that something was troubling me, so she asked if I wanted to share. I gave her a brief summary and she asked if she could speak to my daughter. I didn't see any harm in it, so they started having a conversation. She then asked if we had a picture of him. I showed it to her and also agreed to send it to her in a message.

At this point in the conversation, she mentioned that she needed to step out to make a phone call, but assured me she was coming back shortly. About 15 minutes later, she returned and revealed something unexpected. Her Taekwondo group wasn't just about practising martial arts; they also took it upon themselves to address certain matters. To my disbelief, she explained that she had sent the photo of my daughter's ex-boyfriend to her group and surprisingly, someone in the group recognised him and even knew where he lived. It was incredibly surreal to hear this and I couldn't believe the turn of events. It all seemed too good to be true.

Then, she asked a crucial question: 'In an ideal world, how would you like to solve this matter?' It sounded like she could make anything happen. Who was this woman who sat next to us in a random ice cream shop in London? I was overwhelmed, filled with hope and apprehension. How did I want to solve this matter, really? Given how unlikely it was that this would ever be resolved, this question hadn't even crossed my mind. All I wanted was for this to stop and for us to know he would not be bothering her again. As unbelievable as I found the whole conversation, the hope of having my wish come true, made me utter these words: 'I want him to leave my daughter alone.' She promised to call me the following day and we said our goodbyes.

On our way back to the car, my ex-husband expressed how unhappy he was that I had shared so much personal information with a total stranger. He was telling me off and asking why I had done that. In all honesty, I had no idea. I just did, as if I had to!

The entire situation felt surreal and none of us, including the children, believed that this woman would ever call us. It felt like a prank of some sort. How could she possibly solve an ongoing problem that had robbed us of peace and joy for months? Torn between disbelief and hope, I found myself in a very strange place after that meeting.

The following day, around noon, I received a phone call. It was her, the woman from the ice cream shop and she said: 'Someone wants to talk to you.' I was astounded when I heard his voice. It was him, the abusive ex-boyfriend! He sounded genuinely upset: 'I'm so sorry for everything. I will never disturb your daughter or your family ever again. I promise! You'll never see or hear from me ever again.' Then the lady put the phone on speaker and said, 'He means it, you've nothing to worry about anymore.'

And just like that, our dilemma ended.

This lady came into my life out of nowhere and disappeared in just the same way. I never saw or heard from her again. We were helped in the most miraculous way when we were at a complete loss. I've never experienced anything like it, before or since.

Needless to say, this miracle renewed my faith, which is today stronger than ever. There is a power out there! Whether we see it, believe it or not. Call it Spirit, call it Power, call it God, it is out there, in here, everywhere!

The Lost Ring

In August 2008, we held a yoga retreat in Oxfordshire and had around 12 participants. As part of our program, we ran a Tai Chi session in the garden after our morning walk. We had lunch, talked, rested and had our second yoga session of the day before dinner, as usual. To end a fun-filled day sprinkled with deep conversations about life, we sang and chanted around a bonfire.

When we came back to our room to get ready to sleep at around 11 pm, Matt told me in a panicked voice that he'd lost his ring. We looked everywhere but couldn't find it. He has a habit of taking off his ring when he teaches and I suspected that he had left it on the grass when we came back to the house after the Tai Chi session.

When I told him that I was going out to the garden to find it, he looked at me as if I had completely lost my mind. The garden was about 55 acres and was pitch black as we were in the countryside. I was guided by a strong feeling that it was there and that I would be bringing it back to him. With that conviction, I ventured into the garden. I could hardly see in front of me but I trusted my instinct. As my eyes slowly adjusted to the dark, I took surer steps towards the area we had practised in the morning. At one point, I stopped walking, bent forward and picked up his ring as if I knew exactly where it was, even though I could barely see the ground. I couldn't believe it! In broad daylight, that search might have taken hours, yet here I was holding the ring victoriously in the dark, before I'd even started looking.

When he saw my big smile as I entered the room, he was so delightfully shocked that all he could utter was: 'You witch!'

This experience reassured me to the core, because without thinking or trying to figure out precisely where he'd left his ring, an inner knowing had guided me out into the garden, without a torch, to the exact spot where it was. I like to think that in my own depth, there exists a well of knowledge that can emerge to help me when needed. Such experiences suggest that there must be more to us than we dare to admit. As Marianne Williamson beautifully puts it:

'Our deepest fear is not that we are inadequate. Our deepest fear is that we are powerful beyond measure. It is our light, not our darkness, that most frightens us.'

Feeling Low

It was on a late spring evening that I found myself restless, emotional and unwilling to settle to sleep. An argument with my husband David had left me agitated. I decided to go to the garden with a small blanket, lie on a reclining chair and look up. The vastness of the sky and the way I could lose myself in the glitter of the stars, have always had the power to bring me back to presence and a sense of balance.

As I gazed into space for a few minutes, I felt as small as a grain of sand, smaller still compared to the infinite view above me. My perspective started to shift as, in the grand scheme of things, the unimportance of my stories and worries became clear. I connected to David's mother whom I've never met and is no longer with us. I sensed her loving presence and spoke to her hoping she would, despite her love for her child, understand the reason for my pain – maybe even take my side! The deeper I entered this silent dialogue, the more my inner sceptic dismissed it as mere wishful thinking. In spite of that, I carried on entertaining it a little longer as it was too comforting to let it go.

Still, it didn't take the edge off and I continued feeling uneasy in my own skin. Unwilling to suppress my emotions and sensations, I gave myself permission to fully experience what I was feeling. I had the sensation that my heart was being squeezed tightly in my chest and I felt truly disheartened.

Then, in the stillness of the quiet air, a small white feather like a gift from the sky, gently landed right in front of me on the table. In England – where I live – a white feather is a sign that a spirit is making its presence known.

Could it be that in the depth of the silent night, while all the birds slept, this feather was truly a tiny messenger, a sign? No matter, I smiled at how synchronous the timing was and how powerful the impact of its gentle landing. Its presence led me to believe that I had been heard, understood and that my feelings were validated. It came out of nowhere transforming all that weighed heavily on me and I was able to feel light once again.

We are a speck in the vastness of this universe and while this is true, it doesn't mean that we don't matter. There are moments when we feel a direct connection with the spirit of it all. Life seems to speak to us personally through messengers like this small feather saying: 'It's OK, you're allowed to feel what you feel. I understand. It's OK to be you. I am here!'

I gently took the feather in my hand, marvelled at it and came into the house with a heart full of smiles. My inner conflict had totally vanished all thanks to this soft and fluffy wonder!

At Peace

My son was diagnosed with a life-threatening disease when he was two years old. His circulatory system was unable to bring blood to major organs efficiently, which meant the other systems could not function optimally. He is therefore diabetic and has major issues with his digestive system, often resulting in severe bleeding and excruciating pain. He is now twelve and we have learnt, in the last ten years, to deal with this dilemma in the best possible way. Our immeasurable pain when we see him in distress seems to be balanced with our ability to savour the good times, which are nothing short of heavenly.

Last year was especially challenging. The doctors were unable to stop his bleeding for long, to the point that we were afraid we could lose him. We searched for specialists across France (where we live) and in other countries. After careful consideration, we decided to go to Marseille where a renowned doctor specialises in his condition. I went there with my son alone as my husband needed to be with our daughter. I was very nervous and feared the worst. Each second felt like an eternity as we waited to be seen.

At one point the nurse came to us and asked me for a document that she couldn't find in our files. I didn't have it, but said I could get my husband to email it to her. The moment she started spelling the address aphm…. I knew that everything would be OK and I had no reason to be afraid. I hardly managed to hold my tears back. In French A P is heard as A Paix which means to peace. H M is heard as AshEm which I heard as HaShem (God in Judaism). My sister who converted to judaism often talks about their god – HaShem. Even though I don't share her belief system – she lives a strictly religious life in Israel – hearing the words calmed me deeply. At a time of utter despair, A P H M, A paix Ashem (To Peace Hashem) only meant one thing to me: Trust in God and all will be well.

Whether this was indeed a sign from above or my mind clinging to anything that could possibly help, my sense of safety was restored with an email address. Just like that, from being a nervous wreck, I became this pillar of strength, unshaken and unmovable, able to truly be there for my son.

As it turns out, everything did work out well and the doctor brought my son back to a stable condition. I can't describe the immense comfort I feel by the fact that I was inexplicably reassured during one of the hardest times of my life. Even though, I am not religious, HaShem was in that moment my rock – a powerful mystery that spoke to my desperate heart and brought me back to peace.

The Gift of Generosity

I have been very fortunate to be able to deepen my understanding of the inner martial art of Tai Chi with my Sifu (master). When I was younger, from the age of 17 until my early thirties, he was both like a big brother and a father figure and taught me much of what I know about the body, movement and energy. Much of what I learnt from Shaolin Kung Fu came from this strong, authentic and kind man. Today, both much older in our 50s and 60s, we practise in his back garden and share moments which I cherish deeply.

As a token of appreciation, I wanted to buy him a gift – a book that I had come across and had already bought for myself on Kindle. When I checked the price of the thick printed copy, I was surprised to see it was £41 – more expensive than I had anticipated. I knew I was going to buy it eventually but wasn't sure when. I also knew this month wasn't ideal as I had a lot of outgoings.

I let go of the thought until a couple of weeks later. While driving back from work and listening to Audible, I heard Joseph Goldstein say in his book *Abiding in Mindfulness Vol. 1* something along the lines of: whenever you have the initial thought of generosity, act on it and don't let your mind persuade you otherwise. He argued that what you give out always comes back – sometimes tenfold. It resonated. I knew deep down how true that was. In my early adult life, I had run into financial trouble, going into debt because I hadn't managed my outgoings as well as I should have. I learnt the lesson the hard way. But hearing Joseph, I immediately thought of the book I wanted to gift my Sifu.
That was sign number one.

I went home and, after having a snack, I sat behind my computer as usual to work. Editing Dorna's book was my priority that day and I happened to resume with the story *A Returned Favour* – an account of one act of generosity that was returned (with a little interest) to the giver in an unexpected way. I couldn't believe that this story was also a reflection on generosity – and how the universe reciprocates what you give out. I was starting to feel that I was being nudged to buy the book and let go of controlling my finances so tightly.
That was sign number two.

I was still editing Dorna's book that same afternoon when the doorbell rang and Dorna answered it. She opened the parcel that had been delivered and was overjoyed to see what was inside. We had just received a gift from one of our participants at a yoga retreat. He knew Dorna was exploring a particular subject and had bought us a book on it as a thank you. She showed it to me, beaming and explained why she thought he had chosen that particular book. She was clearly touched.
That was sign number three – and the one that finally propelled me into action.
The urge to send this gift to my teacher just couldn't be denied any more!

So I went straight to Amazon and excitedly purchased the book.

About five minutes later, my phone pinged. It was a note from my old building society, Nationwide (British building society, similar to a bank), where I still had a little money. To my surprise, the text read:

Good news – we're pleased to let you know that £50 has been paid into your account ending 7556. This will appear as The Big Nationwide Thank You.

As unbelievable as it was, it turned out that Nationwide was giving £50 'thank you' bonuses to its members as part of *The Big Nationwide Thank You*, following its acquisition of Virgin Money UK in October 2024.

I was stunned. I had never – not to this day – received money from a bank or building society just like that. It was so surprising and almost unheard of that many people thought it was a scam.

What perfect timing to reinforce Joseph's advice to act immediately on generous impulses and not delay acts of kindness, as it always finds it way back to you.

Candlelight

My mother had been battling cancer for over ten years. Her small body went through so much, but her strong spirit kept her going, showing us the unbeatable power that is beyond the flesh. In the end, she was ready to go. A few nights before she passed, she gave away the jewellery that she had always worn. It was undeniable that the dreaded time was fast approaching. The pain of the anticipated separation was unbearable and we lived in an almost surreal reality. It was as if our feet weren't touching the ground. We were going through the motions but were already taken by a dark and heavy sense of loss.

When she went to hospital, we took it in turns to stay by her side during the night. She was happy with that arrangement as she much preferred not to be on her own. But that evening, I saw something in her eyes that I'd never witnessed before. It was as if she didn't want me around so that she could detach from this world without hesitation. I felt my presence was in the way, but I didn't know what to do. I couldn't just leave and let her go.

The following evening, none of us were allowed to stay over as the nurse came and asked all of us to leave. She must have sensed that my mother needed to be alone. In the early hours of the next morning, we received a phone call from the hospital. They suggested that we go and say our final goodbyes as it was clear that my mother was taking her last breaths. I'll never forget that Sunday morning. Even though the roads were quiet, we wished we could have flown to be by her side. Nonetheless, by the time we'd arrived, she was already gone.

Just like that, my beautiful mother, a kind, generous and warm-hearted being left us, devastated and heartbroken. Shocked by the reality of her death, my father, my two sisters, my brother-in-law, my son, my late husband, a few friends and I left the hospital without uttering a sound. Cocooned in grief, we drove back home. By the time we were back, my parents' house was filled with friends and family who were there to offer their support. We are very lucky to have a tight-knit community to lean on. The house was buzzing with movement while I sat motionless, deep in contemplation. Every now and again, someone would sit by my side, offer a kind word, a gentle touch or their loving presence. Even though I felt and appreciated their love, nothing was more pronounced than a deep sadness that seemed ready to engulf me. In an attempt to bring some light to my darkness, I started speaking silently to my mother in case she might hear me. I said: 'Mum, if it is true that we don't vanish from existence after death, please show me a sign. If you are present and can hear my inner thoughts, prove it to me now.' My inner conversation was interrupted as others started talking to me and I forgot all about my plea.

As I had sat motionless, I'd been staring at an unlit candle tucked away at the back of the TV stand, two shelves below the television. It was almost hidden at the back and on top of it was a glass shelf, decorated with other ornaments. All of a sudden, I saw that it was lit. No-one had gone under the television to light this candle. I was sitting right there in front of it. It was as if the flame had just appeared out of nowhere. I jumped and removed it, as leaving it there could have caused a fire. As I did, I felt a certain energy and knew something was uncanny about this. Initially, I was taken aback, stunned and wanted to share what had just happened, but there were already a lot of intense emotions in the room and I didn't feel it was appropriate to do it then.

As the evening went by, I started to succumb to my sceptical mind even though I wasn't fully satisfied. It was easier for me to dismiss the whole episode than to accept it as a true sign of my mother's presence. Deep down though, I felt uneasy – almost disloyal to what I had sensed and witnessed. Even if I were to consider the unlikely possibility of not noticing someone light it while I was immersed in my thoughts, it was still hard to believe that anyone would light and leave it there. What would be the point to keep it buried at the back of a shelf, hidden from view on a wood/glass unit, where it could crack the glass above and potentially cause a fire?

Once the ceremonies were over, I decided to tell my close family and friends to see their reaction. I was surprised that even those who deny an afterlife of any kind perceived it a sign, especially after I showed them where the candle was.

Despite my own initial reaction and that of my loved ones, I cannot know for certain if it was indeed my mother's light that brought the candle to life. I wish I could know for sure that it was proof of her presence, but how can I? Even if I were given a thousand signs, I would never be completely certain. How can the logical mind ever comprehend illogical and mysterious phenomena such as this?

In any case, it is impossible for me to deny the feeling that came over me as I saw the mysteriously lit candle. Even if what happened wasn't significant in any other-worldly way, I am happy to see it as a symbol. A symbol for the candle that was lit in my heart by my mother's love and her presence *throughout* my life. I will indeed cherish its flame for the rest of my days, knowing its light will forever guide my way.

Her Funeral - Her Voice

Over 20 years ago, when my daughter was in primary school, I met one of the mums while picking her up from an after-school club. This woman, who exuded confidence and appeared well-to-do, happened to be Iranian-British like me. We exchanged telephone numbers in case either of us ran late picking up our daughters. As time passed, we developed a close friendship, enjoying each other's company while our daughters played. This went on for a couple of years. As time went by, it became obvious that my friend was dealing with her troubled past through excessive drinking.

I remember the countless hours we spent on the phone as she poured out the hardships she had endured in her childhood and two failed marriages. It was heartbreaking, given that she was an exceptionally bright woman, full of zest for life and always aiming to better herself. She explored many avenues for self-help, reading great books and getting a degree in her passionate field – Chinese Medicine. Yet, to my knowledge, she never confronted her drinking problem. Unfortunately, it spiralled out of control to the point that it took its toll on our relatively new friendship.Eventually, she moved away from our area and we lost touch.

Fast forward 15 years, one evening, out of the blue, she called me and shared her painful journey during those years. She had fought cancer, had suffered financially as her new business venture had failed and the list went on. She explained that she had returned to the area to be close to her teenage daughter again and asked if we could meet. When I went to see her in her new flat, I was sad and concerned to learn that she had attempted to take her own life six times. She told me how deeply distressed she was each time she woke up in hospital and realised she had failed. As she spoke, she was calm and collected, yet she described an intense anger for being alive. Nothing in our conversation gave me the sense that she had renewed her willingness to live. I could feel that she was still a danger to herself and naturally felt a strong desire to help. The next day, I made a few phone calls to charities specialising in such matters to educate myself on the best approach. Everyone I spoke to, in one way or the other, told me that this was out of my control and if she made that decision again, there was nothing I could do to stop it.

I soon realised that she was still deeply struggling with alcohol and her addiction was completely ruling her life. She called me a few times while under the influence, asking me to help. On one occasion, she wanted me to keep her jewellery as she had convinced herself that someone was going to steal it from her. Given her condition, as heartbreaking as it was to say no, I knew it had to be done. She would often get paranoid during and after drinking and taking her cherished possessions could no doubt lead to trouble. Apart from offering to go with her to AA meetings if she ever chose to take that route, I knew that anything else I would do to attempt to help her, wouldn't tackle the real issue. We had a conversation about this when she was in the right state of mind and she promised that she would contact me once she was a bit more settled in her new place. She assured me that she would take me up on my offer.

She never did.

A few weeks passed and I received a phone call with the devastating news that she had finally managed to take her own life. I cannot express the heartache I felt, not only for her but also for her family – her three children and everyone who had witnessed her dependency. I couldn't believe that this attractive and charismatic woman had spiralled down the way she did. On the outside – when she wasn't drinking – her life was perfect. She had a unique and elaborate way of decorating her home and always wore beautiful clothes and makeup. She knew how to bring people together and have a great laugh and besides, her cooking was out of this world…

But now she was gone.

I couldn't help but feel that all of us, everyone who knew her, were responsible for her passing, yet equally powerless to prevent it. Guilt was asking me: Could I have done more? Had I let her down? Life was answering, it was her call after all.

During her funeral, her teenage daughter shared a moving piece she had written. Following her, a couple of her friends took the stage to share fond memories – one mentioned how much fun they'd had partying together. As I sat there, I couldn't help but notice the absence of any mention of what had happened. There was a huge elephant in the room and I wasn't sure if that was the right way of handling it.

Just as this thought crossed my mind, I felt her powerful presence, as if she were sitting right beside me. It was as if I could hear her urging me to stand up and speak. I had absolutely no intention of doing that, so I ignored the insistent push. She persisted with the same determination and unwavering spirit I had seen in her. 'Get up,' she seemed to say. 'Now, go and say it. Say something.' I must be imagining it, I thought, but eventually I found myself in an unavoidable exchange with her. 'What do you want me to say? I have nothing to say.' She insisted, 'Go and say it. Say it.' What happened next was beyond my intellectual understanding and all my beliefs.

I had never heard or experienced anything like this, ever. Before I knew it, in the midst of this inner conversation, an energy lifted me. It was as though, refusing to accept my resistance, she had somehow managed to eject me from my seat. Or so it felt. I stood and saw my legs walk me towards the stage – I had no control. I remember looking at the movement of my legs telling them: 'What the hell do you think you're doing.' I had nothing to share and no reason to take the stage and yet, I was walking to stand in front of an audience of 60 or 70 people. There was no going back.

When I took the stage and looked at everyone staring at me, I was blank. I stood in the middle of the stage without saying a word for what felt like an eternity. I knew something needed to be shared, whether I liked it or not, so I waited until the words came to me. She had left three children behind. I looked at them and then at everyone present, briefly explaining how I had taken the stage. I had not decided or intended to say the words that followed. 'She wants me to say that she is happy and relieved. She wants to make sure that no-one present, or not, carries the burden of guilt on their shoulders. She is finally where she wanted to be.'

I spoke these words with a power and confidence I had not known in myself – especially during public speaking. It was as though a special strength was granted to me to clearly deliver this message. I saw the relief in the eyes of her children who later told me they had sensed the presence of their mother while I was speaking.

Even though I am used to speaking in public at present, at the time of the funeral, I would have never stood before a crowd, mostly strangers, to talk of such delicate matters. What came over me then remains a mystery. Today, I am certain that those words had to be said and for some reason, I was the one to deliver them.

R.I.P dear friend. We loved you deeply.

Magic Secret

I was in my early thirties when, in 2001, my paternal grandmother passed away. Four years had passed since I'd last seen her. She was in Iran and I had been living in London for over ten years.

That evening, I sensed that something was wrong. I knew that she was being discharged from hospital following an operation on her big toe due to diabetes. I was unnerved even though I had been reassured that she was on the road to recovery. I called her to welcome her home but the line was engaged. I don't recall my grandparents ever spending more than a couple of minutes on the phone. They were of a generation that would rather talk to their friends in person. So after a few failed attempts, I was alarmed. I decided to call my father and ask him if he had any news. When I heard the engaged tone, my stomach wrenched. I could have concluded that they might be speaking to each other, but no. I had an unsettling feeling that something had gone terribly wrong. A few minutes later, my fears were justified; she had passed away while lying down, resting on her bed after she returned from hospital.

I adored her and we were very close. The two of us had travelled together a few times and had created very fond memories. Being the ultimate housewife, she taught me how to knit, crochet and the value of keeping an organised and clean living space. She was strict in some respects but had a great sense of humour and she could make me laugh till my belly ached. I laughed with her, cried with her and poured out all my troubles while she listened tenderly. She always knew what to say or do to make me feel better – her words of wisdom still echo in my mind. Often, when she saw my long face, she'd offer to play games with me or take us shopping. In her company, I knew I mattered and was loved unconditionally. She had a knack for making people feel special and a talent to show her love. Whenever they had guests, which was most of the time, she always made sure to cook their favourite dish. Generous in every way, she was also very liberal for her time. I could indeed write pages and pages describing her. Suffice to say, I was very blessed to have her – Ra'na Joon – as my grandmother.

Not long after she died, a deep sadness came over me when I remembered she hadn't kept her promise to me. When I was a child, she had given her word to share the secret of a game she used to play with us. She would gather children and adults around, make a rabbit using a handkerchief and slip her ring onto one of its ears. Before leaving the room, she would instruct us to pass the rabbit along when she was gone, until someone would decide to take it and hide the ring. When she returned, she would scan the room and uncannily identify who held her ring. How could she do that? It was so awe-inspiring for my young mind. Even as an adult, I was still mystified! Each time we played, I would beg her to tell me the secret but her answer was always the same: 'One day, when you're older.' Now she was gone and that secret could never be told. Through tears, like a child, I complained: 'You promised you'd tell me but you've left and now I'll never know!'

A few days later, I was ironing in front of the television on an early afternoon. A black and white movie, starring Norman Wisdom, played in the background. I wasn't paying much attention until a particular scene grabbed me. He gathered the children around and began making a rabbit in exactly the same way my grandmother used to. He carried on playing the game precisely as she did. I was glued and my jaw dropped when, at the end, he turned to the mesmerised children and asked, 'Now, would you like to know the secret?' They all screamed a loud 'Yay' and I, like a child, felt just as excited. He explained that there is always a stooge in the room, someone who points to the person who has the ring. And just like that, a few days after my sobbing and complaints, the promise was honoured. I couldn't stop my tears.

Obviously, I have no way of knowing if it was truly her spirit that orchestrated the entire set-up: me ironing, watching the scene at the exact time that it was aired. Maybe it was my intense longing that made me tune into the answer. A longing that had nothing to do with the secret of the game but everything to do with the loss of this beautiful being in my life and my inability to ever reach her and connect. That was the source of my pain, but that day, it all vanished.

A doubt was planted and it was now possible to entertain the idea that a communication had taken place.
I then recalled a pact we had made a decade before she left us: Whoever died first was to give a sign to the other, proving that there is more to life than the eyes can see. Was that the sign?
This remains a great mystery!

Easing Resistance

My life experience has shown me time and again that when conflict arises, what I think, feel and sense about the other person affects them and their behaviour towards me, whether they are near or far. I have applied relaxation techniques whenever my relationships have been strained by conflict or resistance. As soon as I become aware of my inner tension regarding the 'other's' actions, I relax my jaw, the back of my neck, arms and so on. Admittedly, it doesn't always result in a complete change of attitude on their part, but it certainly impacts me enough to help me see their perspective and gain clarity.

The mere act of redirecting my energy to myself, noticing how the situation is affecting me in the moment, seems to untangle some of the knots between us. On the contrary, when I stay focused on what caused the tension, feeding it with my thoughts and fuelling my inner stress, the situation usually worsens.

On this particular occasion, I was dealing with someone adept at manipulation and gaslighting. She would say one thing one moment and completely deny it the next. Since I had no other choice but to interact with this person daily, I sensed that I was becoming quicker at reacting internally to her inability to see how her beliefs and actions were impacting us. Focusing on her actions, which I couldn't change, was affecting me and I found myself feeling like a victim. I had unconsciously given her control over my emotions. Seeing the negative effect on my stress levels, I decided to become very vigilant and quicker at noticing my inner energy instead of focusing on her actions. Protecting my inner peace was my job, not hers. It was time to reclaim my power and establish a strong energetic boundary, or I would be at the mercy of someone who didn't have my best interests at heart.

Our situation required regular contact during the day, some of which was time-sensitive. I had sent her a text and she had not responded in due time. As hours passed, I became increasingly concerned about the repercussions of her delay. The moment I realised that I was holding my body tense and sensed my inner fire building, I remembered my intention. It was my responsibility to maintain my emotional well-being, so I redirected my focus to myself and stopped giving her attention and therefore, my energy.

That very moment, I heard my phone ping! She finally replied at the exact moment I had chosen to reclaim my power and prioritise my inner peace. The ping of her message felt like an 'Amen' to my decision. It seemed to me that the universe had just delivered me a message along with hers: 'Keep to your inner pact and all will be well.'

It was the timing that blew my mind. Had she messaged ten minutes later, I would not have seen it as a sign of encouragement and approval.

With renewed resolve, I continue to choose vigilance and catch myself whenever I slip into unnecessary resistance.

No-One Is Proud Of Me

It was a summer's day – 14 June 2022, to be exact – when I sat on a bench in St. James park (London), feeling really sad. I was 26 at the time and even though I had my path set to study for a master's degree in a field of my choice, I felt incredibly sorry for myself. It is embarrassing to admit, but I had this self-indulgent whine running through my head that '*no-one cares about me, no-one loves me, no-one is proud of me.*' I genuinely felt unseen.

Then I remembered someone I had done an internship with, whom I hadn't seen in a while. I wanted to arrange a meet-up with her, so I sent her an email there and then. I had just launched a blog, so I included an article I had recently written, thinking it might be something she'd enjoy.

I didn't expect a reply at all – she is usually really busy and when she does respond, it's normally after a few weeks. But this time, it was different. I sent the email at 4:17 pm and to my surprise, her response popped in my inbox just five minutes later. At 4:23 pm, I opened her email and read: 'Gosh this has blown me away, I'm so proud of you!!!!!!' She then invited me to visit her in Greenwich anytime that I wished.

I was almost spooked that she used the word 'PROUD'. Only minutes before my mind had been stuck in a loop, repeating over and over: '*no-one is proud of me, no-one loves me.*' But then, her encouraging words shattered my false beliefs.

In that moment, I knew this message wasn't just from her. It was Life, Existence itself, showing me clearly that my self-pity had no real foundation. I saw then that *I* had been the one creating a false version of my life, unintentionally drowning myself in heavy emotions. Then, in an instant, with one sentence, I was unexpectedly set back on track!

Ski Trip

This happened about 40 years ago when I was seventeen years old, on a school ski trip to Switzerland. My best friend and I shared a room in a beautiful old hotel.

One evening just before falling asleep, my eyes caught sight of my scrunched-up shirt-bag, lying on the bedside table. The more I stared at the bag the more it looked like Mother Mary. I could make out her head and her robes. Even her arms held slightly aloft – a pose common in many depictions of her.

As I began to tell my friend who, without me realising, had become transfixed by the same strange image, we both exclaimed the exact same words at the same time: 'That looks like the Virgin Mary!'

The moment we said that, the bag (Mary) tumbled over, finally resting on its side. Completely freaked out, we both jumped up, turned on the lights and took the bag out of our room leaving it somewhere – anywhere – away from us!

The next day, as my friend and I were walking outside getting ready for the day's skiing, we found ourselves beside our hotel which was a very old converted church. Underneath what we worked out was our bedroom window, we were taken aback by what we saw…
A large crucifix.

This was and remains, by far, the strangest, most inexplicable moment of my life. Surely too many factors to put down to coincidence.

Why Fear, When I am Here

We faced a big project ahead of us: For over 16 years, my partner and I had been living under the same roof while still renting out our individual flats. Although buying a house as a couple had crossed our minds several times, we never managed to figure out how. It became clear at some point that keeping our separate flats while buying a shared space was simply not feasible. The only viable option would be to sell both properties. Disrupting a well-functioning arrangement was unsettling. While our hearts yearned to own a house together, we were very aware that by doing so, we would be giving up the safety of having our own flats. This joint venture needed us to sacrifice our security blanket.

To say that I was especially anxious about this project would be an understatement. The task ahead of us was immense: We had to move out of our current rented flat, sell not just one, but two flats (including one with a very short lease) and buy a new house. My ambitious goal was to accomplish all of this within a single year. When I shared my plans with friends and family, they thought I was dreaming and being unrealistic. I was told that in order not to be disappointed, I should be expecting to achieve my goals in at least two to three years. As fanciful as it seemed, against all odds, we did manage to accomplish everything in just over a year. The mysterious coincidence I am about to describe gave me the confidence and reassurance I needed for this project despite its bumpy start. It may have even contributed to the overall achievement of the intended deadline as it shifted our mindset.

It happened during the chaotic process of moving out everything from our rented flat into our two separate flats. I couldn't fathom how we had managed to accumulate so much stuff which made our move very stressful. At the time, every penny counted and a misunderstanding with the moving company meant that we not only had to incur the extra charge of £400, but we also had to leave some of our belongings behind and move them ourselves the next day. The physical exhaustion and the emotional stress of dealing with the rude staff of the company brought me to tears.

The next day, we hired a van to move what was left. After returning it, we drove our car to a charity shop to donate a few bags. By this point, both physically and emotionally drained, we mustered every ounce of strength to keep our spirits high and maintain a sense of humour. Although my memory fails me in the exact words, I remember saying jokingly to my other half that we should be paid for the unexpected extra labour in the move.

We arrived at the charity shop, parked the car and started emptying the boot of the car. As I reached for a full bin bag, a small box fell out. Despite my efforts to put it back a couple of times, it stubbornly dropped onto the boot floor next to the bag, not inside it. Frustrated at my inability to do this one simple task, I made a determined third attempt saying: 'This box does not want to go to charity!' Once again, the box slipped from my hands and this time, the impact made the lid open and £200 flew out of the box. I had stashed the money away for a rainy day and completely forgotten about it. My joke was heard! Indeed, we had been paid for our extra efforts and some of the money we had reluctantly given to the moving company, was returned to us!

Yet, the mystery didn't stop here.

Money wasn't the only thing that flew out of the box, among a few other items, there was a small picture of Shirdi Baba. My partner, a devoted disciple of Sai Baba (a spiritual guru and successor of Shirdi Baba), had purchased several pictures of Shirdi Baba during a trip to India. In that moment, it struck me that throughout the entire move, I had noticed, on numerous occasions a picture of Shirdi Baba – be it on paper, a pendant, or a book – had fallen, catching my attention. I hadn't given it much thought until that very moment. Could this be a sign? Why was I being drawn to him? My curiosity grew so the following day, I decided to Google Shirdi Baba and find out if he has a main message. Given that Sai Baba's teachings centred around 'Love All, Serve All,' I wondered if Shirdi Baba shared a similar message. And indeed, he did. His timely message instantly relieved me of all anxiety and worries about our joint project. It read: 'Why fear, when I am here.'

It is my belief that the 'I' that Shirdi refers to is the same 'I' in all of us, that timeless and ageless presence within. His message served as a profound reminder that underneath all the dramas, we are pure awareness. By remaining connected to our deepest Self, to the presence within, we can navigate through any situation without fear and with greater ease. This brought me back on track and what previously seemed like an immense task, suddenly became very manageable. Needless to say, from then on, during the entire project, whenever an obstacle came up and I felt on edge and uncertain, the mantra 'Why fear when 'I' am here' would bring me back to peace.

It may seem like pure coincidence that £200 flew out of a box just minutes after I wished to be paid for our hard work, but its impact was priceless. Perhaps Shirdi Baba's message was also random, yet even in its randomness, it sparked a deep sense of connection and inner peace, miraculously shifting my mindset during a highly emotionally charged time.

With Heart

Eyal, my ex-husband, had just lost his dad and I'd been chanting for him – trying to help ease his journey through samsara (the cycle of life, death and rebirth in Buddhist belief). That same day, I was looking at my mum's picture on the altar – she had passed in 2018. I had this moment of remembering how I used to ask my mum for signs. I thought 'Oh, I forgot, I haven't asked her in ages.'

I looked at the Gohonzon (sacred object of devotion), a naturally-formed piece of driftwood in the shape of a beautiful big wooden heart. It always reminds me of her. So I said aloud 'Mum, I need a sign. Just let me know you're there.'

About an hour later, I set out to walk near my house to do my usual walking ritual. I sat for a while on a low wall just near my door – about ten meters away – and something shiny caught my eye on the ground, just this little silver glint.

I picked it up and started laughing. It was a heart. A little heart-shaped pin. I was laughing because my mum's whole thing – her symbol you could say – was a heart.

Then I turned it over…

It had her name on it '*Peggy*' – my mum's name!

What are the chances? It's not like Peggy is a common name here in Ibiza. It's not a Spanish name! It's not even an English name but rather Irish – a nickname for Margaret.

I asked for a sign and there it was. A heart, in silver, with 'Peggy' on it, lying right near my house.

I had goosebumps all over. It wasn't just random. I don't believe things can just *drop from the sky,* I know how signs work. It's about synchronicity, tiny cogs all moving together to make something happen. Even if that pin had been part of an old birthday card, tossed out years ago and somehow made its way outside – maybe the gardener's strimmer flung it across the garden – who knows? Whatever the reason, it had landed there. I had never seen it before but there it was, winking at me to see it, exactly when I asked for it.

It was so specific. So timely. So *her*.

I took a photo of the pin and sent it straight to Eyal and left him a message. I told him this sign wasn't just for me. Maybe it was also for him from his dad, just not as directly. I don't know if he heard me as his dad's passing was quite recent but I had a feeling that the sign I was holding in my hand was a message for both of us, from the beyond.

It is not the fact that the pin's appearance can or can't be explained that made this experience so moving. It is the fact that it popped up *then, r*ight *after* I asked. Nothing can take that extraordinary moment away, not even logic.

Whispers of the Beloved

The past few years have been filled with sorrow and grief. Right before lockdown, a time when hospital visits were closely regulated, I experienced the devastating loss of my father to brain cancer. Were I to write the story of our reunion, ten years before he passed away, pages of an entire book would be filled. After being separated for over two decades, we found ourselves living together during his final years. Our bond grew stronger day by day and we cherished every moment we shared. I could never have prepared myself for the profound impact of losing my guide, my pillar of strength, my dearest friend.

It was hard enough to lose him but not to have the support of our many friends during the funeral made the grieving process ten times harder. We had, as a family, made the difficult decision to forgo a large funeral in order not to contribute to the spread of Covid-19 . Only a couple of friends, my two sisters, their husbands and children were present. The clouds of loneliness wrapped our home, growing darker by the day and my heart felt heavier with sadness everyday.

Life couldn't get worse, or so I thought. Destiny, however, had another crushing blow in store.

About a year later, my brother-in-law, the husband of one of my sisters, tragically lost his life to a sudden and severe heart attack. I totally lost my inner compass. It was as if I were drowning in the vastness of an unforgiving sea, desperately searching for something to cling to. Giving up and surrendering to despair was not an option; I had to gather my strength, for myself and my two sisters.

For the anniversary of the sudden passing of my brother-in-law, I was given the responsibility to find a poem to read during the ceremony. It was a task that lay heavy on me as I wanted it to be a true reflection of our sorrow after his loss. I spent many nights alone, crying and sifting through many poems in the hope of finding one that was relevant. A couple of nights before the ceremony, I felt pressure building as my many hours of searching for a suitable poem had proved futile.

That night, I had a vivid dream of my late father. His words echoed in my mind: 'Find a USB, there is a poem in it.' When I woke, I pondered whether this was a mere figment of my imagination or if it was indeed a true message from beyond. I knew I had cleared out all my father's belongings, including the drawers in his desk, but I couldn't shake my curiosity. I scoured through every drawer, desperately hoping to find a USB. And to my astonishment, hidden under a stack of papers, I discovered one. I trembled with anticipation as I opened the contents on my laptop. Could this USB really hold the poem I was desperately searching? In disbelief and utter surprise, I discovered four files: Three photos and one document. Two of the photos were of my widowed sister on her own and one of her son.

The document was a poem titled 'The Lonely Lover' – a soulful piece depicting a woman's struggle to embrace life on her own, while refusing to let go of the memories of her beloved.

How was that possible? How could all the four files be related to my sister who was mourning the death of her husband? Why were there no family photos including him? Only two photos of her, alone (the lonely lover), one of their son and not a single one of him. Why would my father have these? What could explain this incredibly relevant poem in the same USB that contained nothing else? Did my father have a premonition while he was alive? I was stunned. I would never know the answers to these questions but I have an overpowering feeling that our departed loved ones can guide us. They are with us and sometimes, just out of the blue, when we are desperate, they manifest their guidance into this reality.

This is the poem:

Lonely Lover

Everything aligns tonight on its course,
Everything is calm..... calm... can you believe it?
I have learned to sleep at night 'remembering you'
Don't worry about me!
I have learned everything!
I have learned to walk in this world without you!
I have learned how to cry silently!
I have learned to silence my sobs with my pillow!
Don't worry about me!!
I have learned everything!

I have learned how to be with you without you!
I have learned...to breathe without you......and to remember you!
I have learned how to miss your absence by dreaming of being with you...
And fill your empty space with memories of being with you!
Don't worry about me!

I have learned everything!
I have learned to laugh without you.....
I have learned to cry without you...and without your shoulders...!
I have learned not to fall in love with anyone else but you!
I have learned not to fall in love with anyone anymore....
And most importantly, I learned to be alive and live with your memory!
But there is still one thing... that I have not forgotten...
how.....!
will I forever erase your memories from the page of my heart...
And I don't want to learn any time....
Don't worry about me!!
I will never learn 'forgetting you'... ~ Shariati ~

Transcendent Caress

I believe it is important to communicate that the story I am about to share contradicted my personal belief system. The experience I am about to describe does not align with my perception of what happens after death. In my worldview when we die, we die as an individual. The drop that we are merges back into the ocean of existence, as energy. The memory of our life, of our story, however, remains part of this ocean forever. The ocean from which all that is born emerges and into which, all that passes away returns. You could say I believe in reincarnation without 'the individual soul' that travels from body to body in different lifetimes. What happened on this occasion though, threw me and my worldview completely. 'Life is a mystery' is indeed the only belief that I can hold onto with utmost certainty.

After a particularly long and exhausting day, my husband and I went to bed. His physically and emotionally demanding job had taken its toll on him, leaving him drained and feeling down. I put my hand on his forehead, softly caressing him. My heart was filled with so much love for him and I could feel it pouring out of my hand. All of a sudden, an unfamiliar sensation started brewing inside me. I felt my hand getting bigger, as big as a man's hand. It was as though an entirely different hand, infused with a foreign energy, had replaced my own. This extraordinary feeling continued to grow in my entire body, pushing my own energy into the background. I was being gently pushed inward, into my own depths, making space for this other presence to take over.

Although I had enjoyed watching Ghost as a movie in my youth, I never really believed that a body can become a vessel for someone else's energy. As irrational as it was, the reality of what I was experiencing was as tangible as the words I now type on this page. From the depth of my being, where I had become a much smaller version of myself, I felt fear rising. I was reassured and *told* that what was happening was safe and there was no reason to panic. With trust in my heart, I completely surrendered. I allowed this phenomenon to unfold without the slightest resistance, embracing it with utter awe and disbelief. Slowly, I embodied the essence of a tall man, unmistakably recognising it as my husband's late father. Pure and unconditional love was flowing as I tenderly caressed him, feeling as though I were a loving father comforting his son. It was an inexplicably strange and extraordinary experience, tainted by peculiar sensations. Yet, despite the strangeness, I felt an immense privilege in being chosen as the channel for a father to reunite with his son.

After a while, the caressing stopped and I was fully back in my body as myself. Shocked, internally quiet and still totally awed.
I heard my husband say: 'That was nice.'
With difficulty, I managed to utter these words: 'It wasn't me.'
As if the entire experience was not strange enough, I could not believe my ears when my husband said: 'I know, it was my dad.'

No words can explain how I felt.

I am fully aware of the scepticism that reading this could evoke. Had it not happened to me personally, I would doubt the sanity of anyone telling such a story. I consider myself a rational person, rational enough to know that my mind alone, cannot comprehend the immensity of this existence. Rational enough to know that despite huge progress, science has a long way to go to explain this kind of occurrence. Maybe one day, a logical reason for such phenomena will be discovered and scientists will not brush them under the carpet labelling them as mad or wishful thinking. But for now, 'inexplicable' is the fairest label I can come up with.

Cultivating Wonder in the Mundane

Having now read through these stories, you may have noticed how moments of wonder – whether subtle or extraordinary – can evoke deep feelings of connection and leave a lasting imprint. These glimpses of mystery aren't just beautiful; they can touch something essential within us. They remind us to stay open, to notice, to listen. It's worth reflecting on how these feelings and connection are not distant or rare – they're accessible to us all, and we can learn to tap into them.

Research into "awe-inspiring experiences" now confirms what many of us have long sensed intuitively: these moments calm the nervous system, promote healing and help us align more deeply with life. Whether through nature, beauty, art, community, love – and yes, the kinds of stories you've just read – they are all an invitation to step into this space.

As Dr. Dacher Keltner of UC Berkeley, who has studied the emotion of awe extensively, writes:

'Awe is mysterious. How do we begin to quantify the goose bumps we feel when we see the Grand Canyon, or the utter amazement when we watch a child walk for the first time? How do you put into words the collective effervescence of standing in a crowd and singing in unison, or the wonder you feel while gazing at centuries-old works of art?'

Awe helps us remember that we are part of a collective whole and moves us away from '*the story of me*'. Therefore, it softens the grip of fear, self-doubt and separation, bringing relief and sometimes insight. Another surprising benefit of awe and a good reason to look for it, even in the smallest wonders (like the twirls of steam from a hot cup of tea), is that it has been shown to be anti-inflammatory!

In summary, the invitation is this: 'slow down and pay attention to details and to the wonder of the mundane.' Take time to savour moments and connect with the life happening all around you.

Often, we are too busy to notice the clouds shifting and changing shapes, but what if we allowed a few moments longer than a glance and a superficial 'aah'? What if we let the feeling really sink in as we watch the magic of existence?

I do not wish to change anyone's worldview. Personal philosophy is what allows us to function in an uncertain world and I honour that. It makes life familiar, comfortable, or inspires us into action. My hope is that these stories have sparked questions, or perhaps helped you remember something you already knew. It is through these values like curiosity and exploration that we begin to discover, understand and eventually, perhaps, find a common ground.

As for me, personal experiences and those of the generous souls who shared theirs, confirm that there is a greater chance of this world communicating directly with us the more we are willing to pause and listen. It is my opinion that we weren't placed on this earth only to survive and suffer. We came here to experience, connect, share and find the unbounded freedom within us. Stephen Hawking (the great physicist) puts it beautifully when he says:

'Although I cannot move and I have to speak through a computer, in my mind I am free.'

This freedom is of a different quality than having control over our actions and being able to do what we want, when we want, in the physical world. It is the freedom of the spirit that can roam anywhere, do anything and even bring about different feelings at will. This is truly empowering, as it enables us to move away from being victims of life's circumstances and stand tall in the Spirit that supports our existence.

Your Story

While I was editing this book for the third time with a proof copy, I pulled a card from Alana Fairchild's deck 'The White Light Oracle'. I never ask for anything specific, but this time, after Donya – my daughter – insisted that I pulled another one, I asked for a card that would tell me how this book will be received. After reading it, I decided to change the existing paragraph to the following quote as it was exactly in line with what I had already written. Another coincidence?
Here what it read:
'Contemplate and briefly describe several moments when you felt joy, gratitude, vitality and aliveness. They may be everyday events or a special event or unusual occurrence. As you record your experiences, you might be able to open your heart with gratitude for those experiences. Perhaps you can cultivate a feeling of wonder and appreciation for how marvellous life can be.'

About the Author

Dorna Djenab was born in France to Iranian parents studying abroad, she spent her early years in Paris and Marseille before moving to Iran at the age of nine, just before the Revolution. Everything changed then.

She had to learn a new language, a new way of life. By ten, she had developed a new identity, no longer considering herself French and Catholic but Iranian and Muslim. That shift was the beginning of a life lived between worlds –between cultures, languages and beliefs.

As a teenager, Dorna experienced the upheaval of revolution and war, growing up in a country experiencing dramatic changes. At 13, fun times included queuing with her friends for rationed groceries and going to secret parties. It was a time of contradictions, risk and joy.

Yoga entered her life at a very young age when her father resorted to the deep relaxation techniques as a way to calm her restlessness. Then again, after one particularly rebellious phase in her teenage years, her father handed her a yoga book with a gentle yet firm instruction to practise. She did – fell in love with the practice and kept going for years. At 16, she had what she can only describe as a moment of seeing *Life* as if for the first time – everything became radiant, vibrant, somehow more real. This high lasted for months. At 19 she began Transcendental Meditation which she practises to this day.

Like many intense experiences though, it didn't last forever. Over time, the clarity faded. The so-called *spiritual high* gave way to fear as she saw many souls similar to hers unable to live day to day life with normality. She immersed herself in the world, living her life as she was *supposed to* and got busy with a career, marriage and motherhood. She stepped away from spiritual practice for a while, unsure if she'd ever return, though the yearning never faded away.

Years later, it came back tenfold. Despite everything that she had managed to achieve, nothing compared with the sense of belonging and joy she had once experienced. The longing was quiet at first but slowly grew stronger.. She could no longer ignore it. She needed to reconnect with what had once felt so immediate and true.

Her enquiry lead her to learn that spirituality wasn't about chasing a state, it was about integrating the depth she had once known into the mundane reality. It was about being deeply rooted in this world knowing that the silent substratum that connects all, is always present.

This integration is what underpins Dorna's work today, teaching yoga, mindfulness, breath-work and self-inquiry. She shares the practices that have shaped her light-heartedly and offers tools for navigating the complexity of life. Her offerings are grounded in personal experience and deep study and are infused with the same curiosity and reverence that first drew her inward. What she teaches supports people not in turning *away* from life, but in *meeting it* with presence, balance and wholeheartedness.

Classes, Courses and More

Dorna teaches yoga, meditation and mindful breathing both online and face to face and offers holistic wellness coaching.

Her current course offerings are:

Jump Start to Wellness
Emotional SOS
Mindful Breathing

These classes along with courses can be found on Dorna and Matt's website:

www.pranasanayoga.com

Both Dorna and her life partner Matt hold retreats in the UK and abroad. They facilitate workshops to increase depth to participants connection to their innermost being.

Dorna also has a Youtube poetry channel which can be visited:
www.youtube.com/@itisnowforever